I PLEDGE ALLEGIANCE

I PLEDGE ALLEGIANCE:

Patriotism
and the Bible

by
PAUL S. MINEAR

THE GENEVA PRESS
Philadelphia

Book Design by Dorothy Alden Smith

Published by The Geneva Press₍ₒ₎
Philadelphia, Pennsylvania

PRINTED IN THE UNITED STATES OF AMERICA

Library of Congress Cataloging in Publication Data

Minear, Paul Sevier, 1906–
    I pledge allegiance.

    Includes bibliographies.
    SUMMARY: Examines various national issues, such as civil
disobedience, amnesty, and segregation, from Biblical perspectives.
    1. Patriotism—Moral and religious aspects.
[1. Patriotism.   2. Christian life]   I. Title.
BR115.P7M543   261.7   74–31489
ISBN 0–664–24819–5

Woe to those who are at ease in Zion
and to those who feel secure
Amos 6:1

These are a smoke in my nostrils,
a fire that burns all the day.
Isa. 65:5

When people say, "There is peace
and security," then sudden destruction
will come upon them.
I Thess. 5:3

I counsel you to buy from me gold
refined by fire.
Rev. 3:18

Contents

PREFACE 9

INTRODUCTION. A Call to Courage
and Candor 11

STUDY

1 American Religion:
Civil or Christian? 25

2 On Commemorating Revolutions 38

3 Insiders vs. Outsiders 50

4 On Civil Disobedience 60

5 Amnesty:
Limited or Unlimited? 72

6 On Ending Segregation 86

7 Rich Nations, Poor Nations 100

(Continued on next page)

8   On the Security-Obsession   114

9   The Struggle
        Against Invisible Forces   127

A CLOSING HYMN   141

PREFACE

This study book was initiated by the United Presbyterian Program Agency, written by a theologian of the United Church of Christ, and developed in consultation with an ecumenical aggregation of seminary professors, pastors, laypersons, and denominational staff. The book is designed in style and method for use by groups of adults and older youth in the churches. It is especially appropriate as a study/action resource during the nation's Bicentennial Era, given the incisive way that New Testament scholar Paul Minear explores tensions between Christian commitment and current American values.

Work on the manuscript began after the 185th General Assembly (1973) of The United Presbyterian Church in the U.S.A. adopted a recommendation that said in part:

> To the extent that we Christians are identified first of all with our nation-state, and only secondly with loyalty to the transcendent Lord who judges all nations, we have difficulty communicating our faith to persons who are critical of or who feel themselves oppressed by the action of our nation. They do not believe us. They see us as "culture-Christians." They reject our testimony to

our Lord, because our real Lord seems to them to be the institution of our nation, or "anti-Communism" or "keeping America great" (at whatever cost to others of God's children). In the Biblical struggle with this transgression, it was called "idolatry." Contrariwise, to the extent that we put down these and other idolatries in the name of the Lord of all, we may be heard gratefully.

David Burnight, a San Diego campus minister who initiated the General Assembly action, said: "Let us simply have a clear look at idolatry, and at the mischief we do with it, in Americanism and otherwise." In that light the denomination's Unit on Evangelism commissioned the author to prepare this study book, and the Unit on Church Educational Services provided editorial assistance.

The manuscript was reviewed and enthusiastically received by a number of persons in other denominations, including those associated with Joint Educational Development and the Ecumenical Task Force on the Bicentennial.

Your reactions to this study book are important. Tell us how you used the material and what action resulted. Write the Program Agency, The United Presbyterian Church U.S.A., 475 Riverside Drive, New York, N.Y. 10027.

JEFFREY C. WOOD
DIETER T. HESSEL

INTRODUCTION

A Call to Courage and Candor

A deep valley separates the complacent congregation from the alert congregation. Both will be found using the familiar hymn "Blest Be the Tie That Binds," but for each the first stanza of that hymn will convey an almost directly opposite meaning. The complacent congregation will measure the strength of that "tie" by the absence of controversy among its members; the alert congregation will test its strength by the ability to face and to overcome inner conflicts. Many Christians assume that the first rule of good churchmanship is: Do not discuss politics here. On entering the sanctuary we tend to mask our faces with smiles. Sociability displaces fellowship. As Halford Luccock used to say, the cross on the altar becomes a bean pot, with the inscription "Don't spill the beans." We may be filled with animosities toward members on the other side of some economic or political barricade, but the church is the last place where we feel compelled to discuss those hostilities. It should be the first.

The first? Yes, if we are to judge by the Bible, whether the Old Testament or the New. From the beginning, idolatries have served as a chief accusation which God makes against his people; and he has discovered those idolatries in the unwitting ways in which his people give priority to national or racial loyalties. Those who try to hide that priority by pious silence have always been the target of prophets and apostles. By stifling conversation out of fear of conflict we all too easily betray a shortfall of faith. To say "Peace, peace" when there is no peace is an act of cowardice and deceit. Such hypocrisy makes us guilty of criminal conspiracy against God, a crime that used to be called idolatry or apostasy. The crime persists, despite the fact that many Christians have ceased to fear those labels.

It has always been true that Christ brings not tranquilizers but a sword. The congregation that seeks peace without justice has already betrayed its covenant with God. To such a congregation Christ's verdict is still: "You have the name of being alive, and you are dead." (Rev. 3:1.) To come alive, such a congregation must break out of its apathy; it must confront its submerged idolatries.

To say this is easy. But to break the habits of amiable blindness, to take the initiative in dealing with suppressed divisions, is difficult and dangerous. Difficult, because congregational habits resist change even more stubbornly than do individual habits. Dangerous, because a sudden eruption of candor can shake the foundations. The release of submerged antipathies can trigger even greater tension.

When a controversy breaks into the open, members of the church may be encouraged to take sides, each side claiming to be right and neither side able to make good its claim. Debates over political matters can generate greater heat in the church than in city hall, perhaps because deeper emotions are involved. If disaster is to be avoided, a climate of confidence must be created that will raise the discussion to a higher level than can be found outside the church.

A climate of confidence—there is the key. That climate can be created only through a fresh encounter with the gospel and its disclosure of the mysterious war and peace of God. Christian faith has its origin in the declaration of peace addressed to all by the Most High God. This declaration has been sealed in the ministry, death, resurrection, and continued presence of Jesus Christ. It has been confirmed by the Holy Spirit in the hearts of those who believe and in the fellowship that makes us the family of Christ.

Wherever the gifts of the Holy Spirit supplant hostility with trust, wherever they become operative in the work of reconciliation, there God is recapturing territory that belongs to him, there he is establishing a beachhead for further penetration of enemy territory. We see the front line of penetration wherever the wisdom and power of God, as disclosed in the cross, subdue their opposites: the wisdom and power of "the world." (See Study 9.) That line is where God's peace is being declared. There the poor receive good news, the blind their sight, and slaves their liberation. There is the genesis of the new Creation, the kingdom of grace. In this kingdom the church of Christ is able to stand firm, to announce peace to the world with candor and courage, and thus to serve as peacemaker.

> The Good News is this expanding and sovereign grace of God in which we stand—*all* of us. For there is *in fact* no other place to stand. In this Good News all in our community receive their vocations within the Body of Christ. . . . [We] are granted stereoscopic vision, so as to be able to see *both* that world in which the elemental spirits take their daily toll, oppressing and dividing hu-

man beings from one another, *and* that world which
God is recapturing for himself.

J. L. Martyn, from an unpublished
mimeographed essay.

Every Christian has been called into the body of
Christ to be a peacemaker. That vocation is accompanied by the gift of joy. Only recipients of such joy *can*
truly serve the cause of peace, and they *must* use the
gift for this end. The same vocation is powered by the
gift of hope: recipients of this gift can and must serve
the same cause. So, too, the gift of trust, confidence in
God's power to overcome every "ruler of this darkness." So, too, the other gifts: gentleness, forbearance,
endurance, self-denial, humility. All are designed for
use in the battle zones. They serve as the arsenal for a
Christian congregation—weapons that prove their
mettle in courageous efforts to deal with its internal
divisions. But they are all instruments of God's peace.
Only those who know that peace, that *shalom,* at first
hand will realize that there *is* a war going on. They will
discern on which front God is fighting; and they will be
able to identify God's enemies, who (as Paul tells us) are
never "flesh and blood" but always the "spiritual hosts
of wickedness." (Eph. 6:10–18.)

In recent years it has become more than ever necessary for churches to apply these peacemaking weapons
to their own inner conflicts, inasmuch as their member-
ships have rapidly become more heterogeneous. So
long as parishes formed like-minded cross sections of a
homogeneous society, the inner tensions could be
managed with a minimum of bother. But that condition
has vanished. No longer is America a melting pot; it has
become a tossed salad. No longer do migrant minorities
become readily absorbed into America, the beautiful;

rather, the cohesive majority has become fractured into a hundred competing minorities, each with a grievance and each demanding greater justice. Each person feels himself a part of some disadvantaged minority, inclined to present a packet of non-negotiable demands to some imaginary majority. The rejection, which is virtually inevitable, pollutes the air with suspicion and pent-up animosity. Breathing that smog, a congregation succumbs to the same lung cancers as do its members.

There is no reason to deplore these changes. They provide a great opportunity for each congregation to fulfill its distinctive vocation, to demonstrate that Christian love which has the power to bind many hearts into one fellowship "like to that above." The Holy Spirit comes not to ratify private bargains between selected individuals and God, but to create communities where believers share all things in common, giving to each whatever he or she most needs. (Acts 2:42–47.) The congregation that represses its internal divisions without seeking to heal them has already turned away from "the grace of the Lord Jesus Christ and the love of God and the fellowship of the Holy Spirit." The congregation is one body to which the proverb "Physician, heal yourself" can be applied.

It would be quite wrong, of course, for a congregation to take account of every type of controversy within its borders. (For more general conflicts, see Speed Leas and Paul Kittlaus, *Church Fights: Managing Conflict in the Local Church;* The Westminster Press, 1973.) It has no business meddling in fights that have nothing to do with its vocation. But, by the same token, that vocation places on the agenda some issues that it has been too disinclined to ventilate. Sometimes, it is the mission abroad that is jeopardized by strong nationalistic loyalty. At other times it is a specific mission within America that is crippled by partisanship and parochialism.

Purpose of This Book

FIRST GUIDELINE

The studies should enable a Christian congregation in the United States to locate within itself those instances of loyalties to the nation which threaten its mission to the world. At what point does the worship of country defy the First Commandment of the Decalogue (Deut. 5:7)? At what point does our ethnicity as Americans destroy our catholicity as Christians? In what ways are we today guilty of idolatry, apostasy, betrayal of our comrades in Christ and desertion of their faith? It should be obvious that within every congregation those questions will prompt contradictory answers. To raise them will provoke controversy, or at least uncover tensions that have been latent all the while. Nevertheless, a candid and courageous discussion of those conflicts should be on the agenda of every congregation.

Of the possible areas of conflict we have selected nine. Some will be especially relevant to your community: allot to them enough time to permit thorough, sustained examination. If the issue is real, it will not yield to anything less arduous. Anything as subtle as idolatry is usually quite unconscious, as American as apple pie. Before we can recognize idolatry in ourselves, our consciousness must be raised; and for that we need the cross fire of criticism from other Christians. The confusion of messianic church with messianic nation has been so prevalent in America from the beginning that a clear concept of the unique vocation of the church cannot be restored quickly or painlessly. Yet that is our objective in these studies.

SECOND GUIDELINE

Each issue should be explored within the context of sustained study of the Bible, that controversial collection of un-American writings. For this reason each of the nine studies begins with a corporate effort to listen to a specific passage; each study ends with a return to that passage, to see what new light the intervening discussion has thrown upon it. Only if this Biblical anchorage for the discussion is taken seriously will it be possible to discern the usually shadowy boundaries between our faith as Christians and our patriotism as Americans. Our attitude toward every modern political conflict may be changed when we approach it from the direction of Scripture, and every Scriptural teaching may also become more potent when we consciously relate it to that conflict. Thus each study seeks to break through the wall that usually isolates our contemporary dilemmas from Biblical accounts of the mysterious ways in which God moves, "his wonders to perform."

The distance between contemporary dilemmas and Biblical accounts may be shorter than we suppose. From Israel's earliest days there were those who viewed God as an ally of the nation, the nation as an ally of God; on the other hand, there were also some who viewed such an alliance as sin of the first order. (A brief summary is provided by Robert Jewett, *The Captain America Complex*, Chs. 1 and 2; The Westminster Press, 1973). Between these two extremes Israel illustrated various degrees of accommodation. Each national policy, then as now, could claim support or resistance in the name of God. Whether or not contemporary readers find ancient texts precisely applicable to modern situations, the discussion of those texts will illuminate a range of contemporary political controversies within the churches.

Christ's Rules of Order

Our aim, then, is to enable congregations to ventilate political controversies by discussing them openly within the context of loyalty to Christ. This loyalty must remain central. It must exert enough centripetal pull to overcome centrifugal forces, however strong. Christ was no American; in him there is no East or West, no boundaries where immigration is denied or visas required. Whenever there is a conflict of interest between Christ and Caesar, the Christian's obligation is clear. It is when two Christians, equally sincere, disagree on whether that conflict exists that their mutual allegiance to the same Ruler requires candid discussion.

Because of this common allegiance, such discussion belongs within the context of communal worship. More is involved than papering over the cracks with sentimental palaver, more than applying skin salve for deep internal injuries. Christian adversaries should participate together in sincere confession of sins, a confession that obligates them to seek reconciliation. (Matt. 5:-23–26; 18:15–20.) Such worship should remind them of their baptismal and eucharistic vows, their covenant with God, their justification by faith which enables them to hope, to love, and to suffer together. (Rom. 5:1–5.) This requires them to listen again to God's commandments and join again in an affirmation of faith, whether old ("I believe in . . .") or new ("God's redeeming work in Jesus Christ embraces the whole of man's

life: social and cultural, economic and political. . . .")
(Confession of 1967, The United Presbyterian Church
U.S.A.). It means that they stand together before the
cross, and acknowledge their common debt to the one
who suffered there. Every effort toward reconciliation,
whether successful or not, becomes their act of worship, praise, thanksgiving, and intercession. Ultimately
it is Christ as reconciler whose presence is embodied in
that action.

Suppose now that a congregation has placed on its
agenda an examination of the conflicts between the
"civil" and the "Christian" religion; suppose it has selected a specific area of conflict; suppose it has engaged
in unhurried and reflective worship. We now ask what
rules of order it should adopt for exploring this sensitive
area?

It should, of course, agree on a common objective.
This goal is more than a restoration of tranquillity, more
than a victory of the more talkative majority over the
less articulate minority, more than a verbalized set of
conclusions that can make everyone more complacent.
The objective should include a more faithful obedience
to the Lord and a renewed devotion to the vocation of
the church. To this end each minority needs every
other minority to help it locate the hidden conflicts of
interest which diminish its own discipleship. If this is
the objective, then the manner in which we proceed
may become as important as the more obvious results.
In meetings for transacting official business we often
consult Robert's Rules of Order, and the more complex
the business the more often the consultation is required. So, in exploring controversial matters where
faith and patriotism excite volatile emotions, it is necessary to apply Christ's Rules of Order:

1. *Repent, the Kingdom of God is at hand.* (Mark 1:15.) The actuality and nearness of the Kingdom requires repentance of everyone. No one can claim immunity; no one should postpone response. It is in deeds worthy of repentance that the power and nearness of the Kingdom take effect.

2. *Seek first the Kingdom of God and his righteousness.* (Matt. 6:33.) To this word *first* there is no qualification or modification. Jesus states an absolute priority in *political* terms: *kingdom.* This excludes giving first place to any other entity: "the church first" . . . "our side first " . . . "America first."

3. *Let your yes be yes and your no, no.* (Matt. 5:37.) This demand for rigorous honesty excludes the desire to please others with soft and bland chatter. The desire for improving public relations must vanish. Trust in one another can only rest on the use of fearless honesty by both.

4. *Beware of the leaven of the Pharisees, which is hypocrisy.* (Luke 12:1.) All disciples need this warning because all are endangered by hypocrisy. The danger becomes greater as the issues become more important and one feels himself more surely in the right.

5. *Ask, seek, knock.* (Luke 11:9.) This triple command has a triple implication for every group of disciples. First, they are in desperate need. Second, they are dependent on God for this critically needed help. Third, they are commanded to rely on him for that help. Group discussion of common problems can illustrate all three.

6. *Be not anxious for your life . . .* (Luke 12:22.) Nothing pollutes the air more rapidly than anxiety

about the future—of the family, the church, the nation. Such anxiety turns every problem into a crisis and diminishes one's flexibility and adeptness in dealing with it. Jesus' command clears the air of this poison.

7. *Judge not, that you be not judged. Forgive . . .* (Matt. 7:1.) Each lash of judgment produces a backlash of judgment, in endless reverberation. The only way to break this vicious circle is to forgive. This does not mean an effusion of "sweetness" but an open, less judgmental appraisal of the merits of the case.

8. *Love your enemies; pray for those who persecute you.* (Matt. 5:44.) Obedience to these commands is always in short supply. Such love is often hidden by sharp words and a brusque manner. Vigorous opposition may be a hidden work of love, infinitely preferable to suave speeches that mask hate. Silent praying is a supreme miracle. Can a person for whom you pray remain an enemy?

9. *Become last of all and servant of all.* (Mark 9:35.) Can a debater obey this command and still argue that only his position deserves to win? How can a runner in a race seek to become last? Yet the command can be obeyed; and when obeyed, it transforms every conflict.

10. *Make disciples of all nations, . . . teaching them to observe all that I have commanded you.* (Matt. 28:19 f.) The two *alls* are decisive. There is no limit to the commission, no exception to the commands. To make disciples is to teach; to teach is to observe; to observe is to receive Christ's promised presence. Eliminate the observance, and the whole sequence evaporates.

As we begin our Bible studies, let us adopt these as our Rules of Order. Their application will make many situations less explosive. Jesus' commands will remind us constantly of the log that blocks our own vision rather than the speck in a brother's eye. This in itself will enlarge the chance for success in the discussions, since a root cause of idolatrous nationalism is concern for the superiority, security, and prosperity of our own in-group. Those who have not been converted away from this obsession have not been converted at all.

Design for Study

It is assumed that each group will select, from the following nine studies, several which will be especially interesting and relevant, although there is no harm in using all nine. Determine in which order these will be studied. (One alternate order to the present arrangement: Studies 6, 7, 8, 1, 2, 3, 4, 5, 9.) Make available to each participant a copy of the book. If all students read it in advance, group discussion is certain to be livelier.

The group will find it helpful to appoint not only a moderator but also a librarian, whose duties will include collecting supplementary resources in advance of the discussion of each topic. In some cases these resources may be found in the local library, following suggestions given at the end of each study. In others, the librarian will want to secure relevant audio-visual aids or recent pamphlets, thus extending the range of the "Voices" to be heard in each area of conflict.

The subjects for study are so complex and the emotions involved so intense that ample time must be allowed for unhurried speaking and listening. A minimum of two hours should be set aside for each session;

some topics may require two sessions. The target is mutual understanding and the quiet expansion of horizons rather than verbal agreement achieved under pressure. At the end of the series (Study 9 is designed as a conclusion of any cycle) one session may well be devoted to taking stock of failures and successes in hitting that target and to assessing how vital the Biblical passages have proved to be in shaping Christian thinking.

A diagram may clarify the six steps which are recommended in dealing with each conflict-area. These steps will take each member full circle, from the Bible to the center of the controversy and back again, from his or her own reflections to the group's debates and back to personal reflection.

1. Each person should listen to the Biblical text in private, reading it slowly at least twice.

2. He or she should then read the exposition of Scripture to establish a baseline for Christian thinking. If there are points in the exposition (summarized in the sentence marked *discovery*) which are unclear or unconvincing, the moderator may choose to begin group discussion with those points.

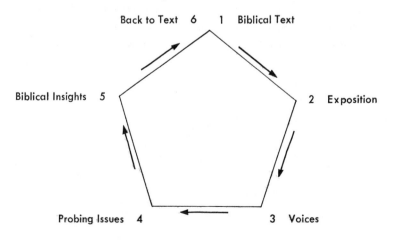

Back to Text   6   1   Biblical Text

Biblical Insights   5   2   Exposition

Probing Issues   4   3   Voices

3. The group should listen together to the *voices*, read slowly enough for the various positions to become clear. This could be accomplished by assigning each *voice* to a participant, to be read aloud.

4. The leader may then invite free and frank discussion of these various positions, probing especially that statement of the issues which divides the group most sharply. In each study several potential issues have been suggested; one or more of these may be used to elicit vigorous controversy.

5. Before the discussion ends, the group should return to the Biblical passage, sharing whatever perplexities that passage may have posed. Several questions are provided which may help to elicit fresh insights into potential collisions between the text and contemporary thinking.

6. After the tumult of open debate, each member should listen personally again to the text, quietly reflecting on what was learned, seeking answers to the more provocative questions, and perhaps extending his or her own search to include other sources.

As each group begins its candid and courageous adventures together, the author of this book says, "Have a good day"—a casual wish, of which a more profound version has appeared on bumper stickers, "Have a good forever."

American Religion: Civil or Christian?

The Scripture: Acts 10:1 to 11:18; 15:6–21

(Consult the Revised Standard Version or the J. B. Phillips translation, focusing on Acts 10:1–5, 9b–15, 19–20, 24–28, 34–35; 11:17.)

The Discovery: God has no favorites

The stories that deal with Cornelius' conversion are unusually long, suggesting that Luke considered them very important. God seems to have had a goal in mind which men kept resisting, and God found it extraordinarily difficult to overcome that resistance. A revolution in attitudes was required, and this revolution involved a cycle of *four* conversions, one after another.

The first convert was Cornelius, a Gentile from Italy, commander of an occupation army (10:1–2). God heard his prayers and issued such directions that, after Cornelius had obeyed them, the Holy Spirit fell on him and on his household. Although he was an uncircumcised Gentile and Peter was a Jew, Peter baptized him in the name of Jesus Christ (10:44–48).

Before this could happen, however, there had to be

another miracle, the conversion of the apostle Peter. This prince of apostles had been bound by firm convictions and practices about holy foods, which governed his association with outsiders, and impelled him to obey the Scriptural rules for God's people. It was far from easy to convert him. His brain had to be washed by a vision of heaven, a request from Cornelius, an angel or two, an explicit command from heaven, the activity of the Spirit, and an emergence of faith among the Gentiles. The key to his conversion was the discovery that God has no favorites. This discovery produced other changes: his attitude toward "the church," toward Scripture, toward the separation of the clean from the unclean (10:28), toward members of other nations, occupations, races, classes, religions. His whole world capsized, so that Peter could never be the same again.

This miracle produced a third: the conversion in the convictions and practices of the churches in Judea (11:1–18). Rumors from Joppa had disturbed these brothers; Peter's vigorous arguments were required to convince them. In fact, they had to hear from God how he had made the unclean clean (11:9). They, too, must follow the guidance of the Spirit (11:12); they must see in the repentance of Gentiles a fulfillment of the promise of Jesus. They discovered that they could withstand God no less than Peter could (11:17).

Later on, Luke tells of an even greater miracle. After the mission of Paul and Barnabas had aroused bitter hostility within the churches, Luke tells how, through Peter's intervention, God converted the company of elders and apostles in Jerusalem (15:1–21). God turned upside down their social prejudices, their theological convictions, their mission policies. The establishment was revolutionized to the point that even "unclean" foreigners could be brought into the house of Israel (15:16–18).

Luke probably told these stories in order to help his readers, fifty years later, to make the same miraculous discovery as Peter. With them, as with almost any people, religion had become a way of cultivating God's favor, of seeking a place among those to whom he will be partial. They count on him to be more concerned for them than for outsiders. To heal such blindness God must ever again use some foreigner or unbeliever. Luke's story thus exerts pressure on all later readers to be converted like Peter from partiality for their own nation. Such conversion is never easy; it is always something of a miracle.

Some Competing Voices

The thrust of the Biblical stories is clear: although God has no favorites, men stubbornly persist in withstanding his impartiality. The following excerpts illustrate various attitudes and convictions shown by Americans, disclosing a possible kinship between American Christians today and Judean Christians in Peter's day.

1892. HERMAN MELVILLE

We Americans are the peculiar chosen people— the Israel of our time; we bear the ark of the liberties of the world. . . . Long enough have we been skeptics with regard to ourselves and doubted whether, indeed, the political Messiah had come. But he has come in us, if we would but give utterance to his promptings. And let us always remem-

ber that with ourselves, almost for the first time in
the history of the earth, national selfishness is un-
bounded philanthropy; for we cannot do a good to
America but we give alms to the world.

Herman Melville, "White Jacket," *The Works of*
Herman Melville (Russell & Russell, 1963),
Vol. VI, p. 189.

1943. SIMONE WEIL

The nation is a recent innovation. In the Middle
Ages, allegiance was owed to the lord, or the city,
or both, and by extension to territorial areas not
very clearly defined. The sentiment we call patriotism certainly existed, often to a very intense degree; only its subject was not set within territorial
limits. . . .

The idea of making the State an object of loyalty
appeared for the first time in France and in Europe
with Richelieu. . . . It was he who first adopted the
principle that whoever exercises a public function
owes his entire loyalty . . . not to the public, or to
the king, but to the State and nothing else. . . . It
was this sin which the devil wanted Christ to com-
mit. . . . Christ refused. Richelieu accepted. . . . His
policy was to kill systematically all spontaneous life
in the country, so as to prevent anything whatso-
ever being able to oppose the State. . . .

The State is a cold concern which cannot inspire
love, but itself kills, suppresses everything that
might be loved; so one is forced to love it, because
there is nothing else. That is *the moral torment* to
which all of us today are exposed.

Simone Weil, *The Need for Roots* (London:
Routledge & Kegan Paul, Ltd., 1952),
pp. 98–99, 109–111.

1967. ROBERT N. BELLAH

While some have argued that Christianity is the national faith, and others that the church and synagogue celebrate only the generalized religion of "the American Way of Life," few have realized that there actually exists alongside of and rather clearly differentiated from the churches an elaborate and well-institutionalized civil religion in America. . . .

Although matters of personal religious belief, worship, and association are considered to be strictly private affairs, there are, at the same time, certain common elements of religious orientation that the great majority of Americans share. . . . This public religious dimension is expressed in a set of beliefs, symbols, and rituals that I am calling the American civil religion. The inauguration of a president is an important ceremonial event in this religion.

. . . I am not at all convinced that the leaders of the churches have consistently represented a higher level of religious insight than the spokesmen of the civil religion. . . .

Behind the civil religion at every point lie Biblical archetypes: Exodus, Chosen People, Promised Land, New Jerusalem, Sacrificial Death and Rebirth. But it is also genuinely American and genuinely new. It has its own prophets and its own martyrs, its own sacred events and sacred places, its own solemn rituals and symbols. It is concerned that America be a society as perfectly in accord with the will of God as men can make it, and a light to all the nations.

Robert N. Bellah, in William G. McLoughlin and Robert N. Bellah (eds.), *Religion in America* (Houghton Mifflin Company, 1968), pp. 5, 6, 14, 20.

1956. ANONYMOUS

An American legionnaire absolutely refuses to come to church now that we have voted that in the sanctuary our flags will be placed so that the position of honor is occupied by the Christian flag instead of the American flag. . . . Let me tell you about our early service on the third of July. It is customary for the congregation to remain seated during the singing of the second hymn. Well, I just about had a rebellion on my hands because I did not ask the people to stand up this time. The hymn was "America the Beautiful." It's perfectly all right, apparently, to sit down for "Our God, Our Help in Ages Past," but irreverent to do so when we sing about our nation. Incidentally, I have noticed for a number of years that congregations sing patriotic hymns with more spirit than almost any other hymns. Even men and women who usually don't sing at all join in. Is this because these songs are so much better known than any others? I don't think so. It is because our nation is a very real object of love and devotion while God seems vague and unreal. When we sing a patriotic hymn the feeling surges through us that we belong to some-

thing great and powerful, but when we sing about
God or Christ or the Church we aren't so sure.

> An Ohio minister's letter in Cornelius Loew,
> *Modern Rivals to Christian Faith* (The
> Westminster Press, 1956), pp. 43–44.

1973. THEODORE M. HESBURGH, C.S.C.

The unity of mankind must be the wave of the
future if we are not to divide ourselves unneces-
sarily according to race, religion, color, sex, and
age, and thereby make human life impossibly complicated aboard our shrinking spacecraft. . . . The
one great remaining divider of humankind, perhaps the worst of all, [is] national sovereignty. Suppose that an intelligent and cultured visitor from
another solar system were to be informed, on seeing our planet as the astronauts saw it from the
moon, that . . . mankind on earth insisted on governing our spaceship by dividing it into 150 different nationalities, some very large, some impossibly
small, and quite a few in between. Our interplane-
tary visitor would also learn that there was no rea-
sonable rationale for these national divisions, that
they often represented people of the same language, religion, race and culture, and were, in fact,
often separated only by historical accidents. Now
that the political separation is a fact, they are ready
to fight to the death to maintain their national
identities. . . .

What I would suggest is that everyone in the
world would be allowed to hold dual citizenship—
to be a citizen of the nation in which he or she
happens to be born, and, in addition, to be able to

qualify for world citizenship. The application to be a citizen of the world . . . would involve certain commitments:

1. One would have to certify his or her belief in the unity of mankind, in the equal dignity of every human being, whatever his or her nationality, race, religion, sex or color.
2. One would have to certify his or her willingness to work for world peace through the promotion and practice of justice at home and abroad.
3. One would have to do something to prove the sincerity of these beliefs, something to promote the peace and well-being of his or her fellow-beings at home and abroad.

> Theodore Hesburgh, Harvard University
> Commencement, 1973.

1935. FRANCIS P. MILLER

The plain fact is that the domestication of the Protestant community in the United States within the framework of the national culture has progressed as far as in any western land. The degradation of the American Protestant church is as complete as the degradation of any other national Protestant church. The process of degradation has been more subtle and inconspicuous, but equally devastating in its consequences for faith.

> Francis P. Miller, in H. Richard Niebuhr,
> Wilhelm Pauck, and Francis P. Miller, *The
> Church Against the World* (Willett, Clark &
> Company, 1935), p. 102.

1915. KARL BARTH

Everything that has to do with the State is taken a hundred times more seriously than God.

Karl Barth, Letter to Eduard Thurneysen, in James D. Smart, *Revolutionary Theology in the Making* (John Knox Press, 1964), p. 34.

Probing the Issues

—As background for group discussion, each member of the group may answer the following questions, circling one of the four attitudes: SA *(strongly agree);* A *(agree);* D *(disagree);* SD *(strongly disagree).*

1. America is today a blessing to mankind throughout the world.   SA A D SD
2. America's wealth was gained largely by oppressing black people, the poor, and foreigners.   SA A D SD
3. The Christian should support or not support his national government depending on his discernment of God's judgment on it.   SA A D SD
4. Nationalism and national pride is a strong hindrance to the work of the Christian church in today's world.   SA A D SD

To compare these responses with a larger sample of opinion, the following data are presented: In a study of the United Presbyterian Church, with statement 1, above, 33 percent of 572 ministers either agreed or strongly agreed while 49 percent of 796 laymen agreed or strongly agreed. With statement 2, above, 12 percent of the laymen agreed, and 27 percent of the ministers. With statement 3, above, 76 percent of the ministers agreed and 55 percent of the laymen. With statement 4, above, 78 percent of the ministers agreed, compared with 35 percent of the laymen.

So the group may wish to initiate discussion by dealing with those statements on which there are major clashes of opinion among its members, or by analyzing the degree of agreement between the group and the larger sample, or by asking why there should develop such a contrast in the attitudes between clergy and laity in American churches.

—A second alternative in procedure is to select those competing voices which attract the strongest support or dissent within the group, for example, Hesburgh or the Ohio legionnaire? Members may be invited to indicate the ground for their dissent or support.

—What contemporary voices echo Melville's picture of confidence in America? Are these voices Christian or non-Christian? Radical or conservative?

—How do the festivals in your town illustrate Bellah's description of civil religion? To what extent are the churches involved in these festivals?

—Do these celebrations illustrate the type of corruptions against which Miller and Barth warn? What are the clearest contemporary signs of that corruption?

—Father Hesburgh mentions three commitments necessary for world citizenship. To what extent has every Christian (and every congregation) in principle accepted these commitments? Does faith in the catholicity of the church necessarily include that kind of citizenship?

—Simone Weil speaks of a "moral torment." What does she mean? Where in your town or among your acquaintances may such a torment be detected?

—Which of the following hymns best reflects each of the *voices?*
> "In Christ There Is No East or West"
> "O Beautiful for Spacious Skies"
> "In the Cross of Christ I Glory"
> "God of Our Fathers, Known of Old"
> "These Things Shall Be: a Loftier Race"
> "We Shall Overcome"

On Rereading the Stories of Peter and Cornelius

—Why did Peter find it so difficult to accept the fact that God has no favorites? Are there legitimate exceptions to this declaration? Was Cornelius himself an exception? If so, was this before or after his conversion? Can the god of any nation actually be a god who is not partial to that nation?

—Compare the attitudes of the Judean churches in Acts, ch. 11, to the attitudes characteristic of American civil religion.

—In what way does this civil religion furnish obstacles to evangelism comparable to those represented by Peter and by the Christian leaders in Jerusalem? How do these obstacles operate in your community?

—Luke seems to have placed a heavy emphasis upon the conversion of Cornelius, yet few Christians today consider conversion to be all that important. What may explain this change in views of conversion? Why is true conversion always miraculous?

—Did the early churches remain nation-blind and color-blind after the conversions in Acts, chs. 10; 11; 15? If not, what should we learn from their reversion to earlier blindness?

Supplementary Reading

On the Scripture

Barclay, William, *The Acts of the Apostles* (The Westminster Press, 1953), pp. 81–92, 120–128.

Foakes-Jackson, Frederick J., *The Acts of the Apostles* (Richard R. Smith, 1931), pp. 87–98.

Macgregor, G. H. C., "The Acts of the Apostles," *The*

Interpreter's Bible (Abingdon Press, 1954), Vol. IX, pp. 131–144, 198–204.

On the Questionnaire

For copies of the complete questionnaire, with the results of a nationwide survey of the United Presbyterian Church, write Dr. Dean R. Hoge, Sociology Department, Catholic University, Washington, D.C. 20017.

On American Civil Religion

Jewett, Robert, *The Captain America Complex* (The Westminster Press, 1973).

McLoughlin, William G., and Bellah, Robert N. (eds.), *Religion in America* (Houghton Mifflin Company, 1968).

Marty, Martin E., *Righteous Empire* (The Dial Press, Inc., 1970).

Michaelsen, R., "Americanization: Sacred or Profane Phenomenon?" in Martin E. Marty and Dean G. Peerman, *New Theology No. 9* (The Macmillan Company, 1972), pp. 91 ff.

On Commemorating Revolutions

The Scripture: Matthew 23:23–39

(Consult the Revised Standard Version or the Jerusalem Bible.)

The Discovery: Hypocrisy blinds, and then it kills

No one enjoys being called a hypocrite. Call a person a heretic or sinner and at most he will shrug his shoulders; but call him a hypocrite and he may get violent. The same hatred for this epithet was true in Jesus' day, so when we observe how frequently he used it, we should ponder why.

Three reasons, among others, might be suggested. For one thing, the sin is almost universally detested; no one likes to be deceived by another's "false face." For another, the affliction is almost always unconscious; the sick man needs shock therapy to become aware of it. Finally, Jesus was almost always concerned about the threat of this disease to his own followers, who needed the sternest kind of warning.

To help them diagnose themselves he proposed a series of tests. The "speck" test, for example: do I spend my time finding and removing the speck from another's eye? (Matt. 7:5.) The "hunger" test: do I give priority to satisfying my own hunger? (Matt. 24:51.) And the "teacher" test: Am I so absorbed in teaching others that no energy is left for my own practice? (Matt. 23:3.)

The text at hand offers three other aids to diagnosis. There is the "big contributor" test for those folk who support philanthropic causes with their money, even to a tenth of their income. And the "public image" test for those who preen in their public mirror, considering good public relations as preferable to private and secret integrity (23:25–26; 6:1–18). The "whitewash" test is similar. On the surface all is clean, respectable, beautiful, since I am a good citizen and church member. No one is allowed to smell the stench of death inside the tomb (23:27 f.).

Finally Jesus describes the hypocrisy which is most dangerous of all because it is so well camouflaged. Matthew places it last in a series of seven, and devotes eleven verses to its diagnosis (23:29–39). Here Jesus used the "anniversary speech" test. The sickness develops in two stages: building impressive monuments to ancient heroes, then giving oratorical speeches in their honor. It could be called the "boomerang" test, since the praise of heroes adds to the credit of the speakers. Or it could be called the "mirror" test, since, on looking into the mirror, cowards can see brave men looking out. So beautiful is the monument, so glowing the speech, that the celebrants forget who they are. Actually their current complacency makes them sons of the persecutors, but by sleight of mouth they are able to pose as sons of the persecuted, fooling themselves completely.

Jesus applied other criteria. He did not trust the monuments or the anniversary rituals which so often dishonor the heroes honored. Rather he judged leaders by their treatment of contemporary troublemakers. He judged a city by its eagerness to welcome the coming liberator (23:39). Ancient heroes are best honored by the welcome given to their successors. Strong medicine, this; but will the disease yield to aspirin?

Voices Ancient and Modern

American history and church history are not the same. The American Revolution may not be viewed as a major event in the history of the church. In Matt., ch. 23, Jesus was speaking of ancient prophets, and not of the heroes of the War of Independence. Even so, there may be comparable risks in celebrating their achievements. It is possible, therefore, to detect certain resemblances between the situation in Matt., ch. 23, and attitudes reflected in the following voices.

1776. THE DECLARATION OF INDEPENDENCE

We hold these truths to be self-evident, that all men are created equal, that they are endowed by their Creator with certain unalienable Rights, that among these are Life, Liberty and the pursuit of Happiness.—That to secure these rights, Governments are instituted among Men, deriving their just powers from the consent of the governed,— That whenever any Form of Government becomes destructive of these ends, it is the Right of the People to alter or to abolish it, and to institute new Government, laying its foundation on such principles, and organizing its powers in such form, as to them shall seem most likely to effect their Safety and Happiness.

1776. JOHN ADAMS

. . . [This day, July 4, 1776] will be the most memorable moment in the history of America. I am apt to believe that it will be celebrated by succeeding generations as the great anniversary Festival. It ought to be commemorated, as the day of deliverance. . . . It ought to be solemnized with pomp and parade, with shows, games, sports, guns, bells, bonfires, and illuminations, from one end of this continent to the other, from this time forward, forevermore.

ca. 1855. FREDERICK DOUGLASS

What to the American slave is your Fourth of July? I answer, a day that reveals to him more than all other days of the year the gross injustice and cruelty to which he is the constant victim. To him your celebration is a sham; your boasted liberty an unholy license; your national greatness, your sound of rejoicing are empty and heartless; your denunciation of tyrants, brass-fronted impudence; your shouts of liberty and equality, hollow mockery; your prayers and hymns, your sermons and thanksgivings, with all your religious parades and solemnity, are to him mere bombast, fraud, deception, impiety, and hypocrisy—a thin veil to cover up crimes which would disgrace a nation of savages.

Frederick Douglass, quoted in Joint Strategy
and Action Committee, *Grapevine*,
March 1974, p. 2.

1776. SAMUEL WEST

As our duty of obedience to the magistrate is founded upon our obligation to promote the general good, our readiness to obey lawful authority will always arise in proportion to the love and regard that we have for the welfare of the public; and the same love and regard for the public will inspire us with as strong a zeal to oppose tyranny as we have to obey magistracy. Our obligation to promote the public good extends as much to the opposing every exertion of arbitrary power that is injurious to the state as it does to the submitting to good and wholesome laws. No man, therefore, can be a good member of the community that is not as zealous to oppose tyranny as he is ready to obey magistracy. . . . Unlimited submission and obedience is due to none but God alone . . . to suppose that he has given to a set of men power to require obedience to that which is unreasonable, cruel and unjust is robbing the Deity of his justice and goodness, in which consists the peculiar glory of the divine character, and is representing him under the horrid character of a tyrant.

Samuel West, Election Sermon, Dartmouth,
Massachusetts, May 29, 1776.

July 4, 1970. DECLARATION BY CONCERNED BLACK CITIZENS

When in the course of Human Events, it becomes necessary for a People who were stolen from lands of their Fathers, transported under the most ruthless and brutal circumstances 5,000 miles to a strange land, sold into dehumanizing slavery, emasculated, subjugated, exploited and discriminated against for 351 years, to call, with finality, a halt to such indignities and genocidal practices—by virtues of the Laws of Nature and of Nature's God, a decent respect to the Opinions of Mankind requires that they should declare their just grievances and the urgent and necessary redress thereof.

We hold these truths to be self-evident, that all Men are not *only* created equal and endowed by their Creator with certain unalienable rights among which are, Life, Liberty and the Pursuit of Happiness, but that when this equality and these rights are deliberately and consistently refused, withheld or abnegated, men are bound by self-respect and honor to rise up in righteous indignation to secure them.

. . . We have warned our White Brethren from time to time of Attempts by their Structures of Power to extend an unwarranted, repressive Control over us. We have reminded them of the Circumstances of our Captivity and Settlement here. We have appealed to their vaunted Justice and Magnanimity, and we have conjured them by the Ties of our Common Humanity to disavow these Injustices, which would inevitably interrupt our Connections and Correspondence. They must have been deaf to the voice of Justice and of Humanity. We must, therefore, acquiesce in the Necessity which hereby announces our Most Firm Commitment to the Liberation of Black People, and hold the Institutions, Traditions and Systems of the United States as we hold the rest of the societies

of Mankind, Enemies when Unjust and Tyrannical,
when Just and Free, Friends.

A Declaration by Concerned Black Citizens in
Black Churches, Schools, Homes, Community
Organizations and Institutions assembled.

1971. WILLIAM STRINGFELLOW

Jesus was a revolutionary. Barabbas was a revolutionary. But the two are distinguished from one another. . . . This issue is dramatized, for us Americans today, poignantly in the American Revolution which, from the New Testament perspective, was a revolution of Barabbas and not a revolution of Christ, despite what either Pilgrims or politicians have said. We who are Americans witness in this hour the exhaustion of the American revolutionary ethic. Wherever we turn, that is what is to be seen: in the ironic public policy of internal colonialism symbolized by the victimization of the welfare population, in the usurpation of federal budget . . . by an autonomous military-scientific-principality, by the police aggressions against black citizens, by political persecutions of dissenters, by official schemes to intimidate the media and vitiate the First Amendment, by cynical designs to demean and neutralize the courts. Yet the corruption of the American revolutionary ethic is not a recent or sudden problem. It has been inherent and was, in truth, portended in the very circumstances in which the Declaration of Independence was executed. To symbolize that, white men who subscribed to that cause, at the same time countenanced the institutionalization in the new nation

of chattel slavery and many were themselves owners of slaves. That incomprehensible hypocrisy in
America's revolutionary origins foretells the contemporary decadence of the revolutionary tradition. . . .

There are no doubt some serious distinctions to
be kept between Rome and America or between
the Nazi State and the United States or, for that
matter, between Revolutionary America and contemporary America; but such issues must not ob-
scure the truth that every civil power shares a sin-
gular characteristic which outweighs whatever
may be said to distinguish one from another. And
it is *that* common attribute of the State as such to
which the New Testament points where the texts
deal with Christ being condemned as criminal.

William Stringfellow, in William Stringfellow
and A. Towne, *Suspect Tenderness* (Holt,
Rinehart & Winston, Inc., 1971), pp. 62–65, 73.

1973. REPORT IN "NEWSWEEK"

In 1973, a bicentennial celebration of the Boston
Tea Party was staged in Boston Harbor. As a cli-
max, the official committee planned for 60 colo-
nists dressed as Indians to dump tea into the harbor. The Sierra Club protested the pollution of the
water. The Indian Council opposed the Indian
dress. The People's Bicentennial Commission,
making the point that ancient rebellions are best
honored by modern protests, dumped oil barrels
overboard in symbolic attack on oil company
profits, and in response to the cry "Down with
King George" yelled "Down with King Richard."

The church of Scientology distributed leaflets, while another group *waved* placards: "Taxation is theft." Peddlers sold balloons inscribed "Happy Holiday."

Cf. report in *Newsweek*, December 31, 1973, p. 12.

Probing the Issues

A group may adopt the role of a committee authorized to plan the celebration of the Bicentennial in its locality. A first step would be to decide which events in 1775, 1776, and 1777 should be celebrated. A second step is to discuss the most appropriate forms of celebration. For instance, what forms of action would fittingly honor the following heroes:

Benjamin Bache: "Let the history of the federal government instruct mankind that the mask of patriotism may be worn to conceal the foulest designs against the liberties of the people."

Thomas Jefferson: "The spirit of this country is totally adverse to a large military force."

Abigail Adams: "If particular care and attention are not paid to the ladies, we are determined to foment a revolution and will not hold ourselves bound to obey any laws in which we have no voice or representation."

James Madison: "The most common and durable source of faction has been the various and unequal distribution of property."

Josiah Quincy: "It is much easier to restrain liberty from running into licentiousness than power from swelling into tyranny and oppression."

—If Frederick Douglass or Abigail Adams were to plan the celebrations in your locality, how do you think they would proceed?

—Or the group may choose to adopt another role, that of a committee appointed to determine whether and how the *church* should commemorate the same events. In that case it may well ask itself such questions as the following:

How is American independence related to Christian freedom?

How is the American Revolution related to the revolution of Barabbas or the revolution of Christ? (Cf. William Stringfellow.)

In what sense does each of these revolutions continue to be a reality today? How does a person participate in each?

In commemorations of this sort how may the hypocrisies of Matt., ch. 23, be avoided?

On a Fresh Reading of Matt., ch. 23

Just as some members of each group will have defended positions which others attacked, so let the group try to formulate a defense for the Pharisees. What might they have said in Matt. 23:30 which would have exempted them from Jesus' attack?

It may be said that every meeting for Christian worship is a form of commemorating the deeds of ancient prophets, apostles, and martyrs—and also the life, death, and resurrection of the Messiah Jesus himself. Even the reading of Matt., ch. 23, as Holy Scripture is part of this celebration. How may this worship be protected from, or purged of, the forms of hypocrisy of which Jesus speaks in that chapter?

If we take a traditional hymn such as the Te Deum or the Magnificat and compare it to "The Star-spangled Banner," how may we determine the hypocrisy-quotient in each, as measured by the tests in Matthew?

To what extent does Matt., ch. 23, illustrate the Jesus revolution of which Stringfellow speaks, in contrast to the Barabbas revolution? From this passage (and our group discussions) for what reasons did the establishment of that day free Barabbas, but not Jesus?

Matthew gives a climactic place to the saying about Jerusalem in 23:37. Did that Jerusalem cease to exist after its destruction in A.D. 70? If not, where may it be located today? In the America of William Stringfellow? How is our group related to that city?

How patriotic was Jesus . . . or how was he patriotic?

Supplementary Reading

On the Scripture

Franzmann, Martin H., *Follow Me: Discipleship According to St. Matthew* (Concordia Publishing House, 1961), pp. 157–172.

Johnson, Sherman E., and Buttrick, George A., "The Gospel According to St. Matthew," *The Interpreter's Bible* (Abingdon Press, 1951), Vol. VII, pp. 528–541.

Trilling, W., *The Gospel According to St. Matthew* (Montreal: Palm Publishers Press Services, Ltd., 1969), Vol. 2, pp. 169–184.

On the Celebration

Handy, Robert T., *A Christian America* (Oxford University Press, 1971).

Hudson, Winthrop S. (ed.), *Nationalism and Religion in America* (Harper & Row, Publishers, Inc., 1970).

Publications of

Ecumenical Task Force, National Council of Churches, Room 576, 475 Riverside Drive, New York, N.Y. 10027.

People's Centennial Commission, 1346 Connecticut Avenue, N.W., Washington, D.C. 20036.

Insiders vs. Outsiders

The Scripture: Luke 4:16–30

(Consult the Revised Standard Version or the New English Bible.)

The Discovery: This liberation is not for us

Here is Jesus' keynote speech in his hometown. Attention soon turns from Jesus' message to the response of his neighbors. That response and Jesus' reaction to it elicit the following chain of inferences. Let the group test each link in the chain; if the links hold, the conclusions would appear to be inescapable.

1. Jesus' message contained "gracious words" for a particular audience at a particular time.

2. As long as his neighbors believed that this was a promise of grace to them, they spoke well of him.

3. But Jesus had the courage to draw a sharp contrast between the residents of Capernaum and those of Nazareth, indicating thereby that he had given priority to the first.

4. As a precedent for this preference, Jesus appealed

to the prophet Elijah, who, during a great famine, had fed not the strong but a helpless widow, not an Israelite but an enemy Sidonian.

5. As a second precedent he appealed to the prophet Elisha, who had helped not the respectable but a despised leper, not an Israelite but an enemy Syrian.

6. Jesus' work in Capernaum, as defended by these precedents, aroused hot anger among his Nazareth neighbors; and they attempted to lynch him.

7. Jesus found this rejection not at all surprising, but fully in line with the customary treatment of prophets, who always seem to insiders to give priority to outsiders, to "them" rather than to "us."

8. The story thus uncovers as the root of this murderous anger—men's instinctive patriotism, the self-interest by which Nazarenes asserted their rights and claims over the Capernaums.

9. Such loyalty to Nazareth had a triple result: it made it impossible for healing by Jesus to take place, it prevented Nazarenes from sharing in his work for others, it turned them into his deadly enemies.

10. In retelling this story Luke was interested not only in the Nazarenes but in his own readers, whom he saw as equally vulnerable to the egoism of the Nazarenes, and subject to the same potential results.

11. The story therefore exerts pressure on later readers to see themselves as potential descendants either of Luke's original audience, or of the Nazarenes at the time of Jesus, or of the Israelites at the time of Elijah.

12. Accordingly how Christians use the pronouns "we" and "they" becomes a matter of salvation or damnation, not only in reading this text but in responding to modern descendants of the prophets.

Some Christian Voices

When we think "we" and "they," we draw a line between insiders and outsiders. Do we draw that line in the right place? The following voices suggest the different places where the line is being drawn or should be drawn.

1963. MARTIN MARTY

The massive silhouette the churches (Catholic as well as Protestant) create on the American skyline is that of a self-preservative institutionalism. The clergyman exists as a promoter of the organization. . . . Since the institutional self-interest preoccupies the churches and does not directly serve the community, it seems to incarnate irrelevance.

Martin Marty, quoted in William G.
McLoughlin and Robert N. Bellah (eds.),
Religion in America (Houghton Mifflin
Company, 1968), p. 342.

1964. RICHARD SHAULL

Theologically speaking, the church may be a missionary community. In actual fact, however, it has become a major hindrance to the work of mission. The local congregation pulls people out of the world and absorbs their time in a religious program rather than setting them free for their mission in the world.

Richard Shaull, quoted in McLoughlin and
Bellah (eds.), *Religion in America*, p. 342.

1956. A PUBLIC OPINION SURVEY

The tendency to put the nation above everything else makes a powerful impact on the moral judgments of Americans, even on the judgments of persons who are not consciously or actively superpatriotic. This impact can be seen in the results of a poll reported in the *Ladies' Home Journal*.

1. Do you love persons belonging to a different religion?
   90% said yes; 5% said no.
2. Do you love members of another race?
   80% said yes; 12% said no.
3. Do you love your business competitors?
   78% said yes; 10% said no.
4. Do you love members of a political party that you think is dangerous? (Obviously the Communist Party was implied in this question.)
   27% said yes; 57% said no.
5. Do you love enemies of this nation?
   25% said yes; 63% said no.

Cornelius Loew, *Modern Rivals to Christian Faith* (The Westminster Press, 1956), pp. 46–47.

1897. SIDNEY L. GULICK

Christianity is the religion of the dominant nations of the earth. . . . In due time it will be the only religion in the world. . . . No peoples have been so controlled by the religion of Jesus Christ as the Anglo-American. No peoples have absorbed it so fully into their national life, and have so embodied it in their language and literature and government. No peoples, as a natural consequence, have so succeeded in establishing prosperous, self-governing colonies and nations. . . . God means that the type of religion and civilization attained by the Anglo-Saxon race shall have, for the present at least, the predominating influence in moulding the civilisation of the world. And everything points to the growing predominance of the Christian religion and Christian civilisation.

Sidney L. Gulick, quoted in Robert T. Handy, *A Christian America* (Oxford University Press, 1971), p. 123.

1974. FREDERICK R. WILSON

. . . [This is] a situation I faced in Tabriz, Iran, in 1954–55, when the CIA's presence and power in Iran was only beginning to be generally recognized (thanks in part to a story in *Saturday Evening Post* by the Alsop brothers describing how the CIA had masterminded and controlled the "spontaneous" overthrow of Mossadegh). I spent nearly a year teaching and talking with a young radical student who had explored many options and was testing the Christian faith. He disappeared for almost a year without explanation; and when he returned and sought baptism, he responded to my inquiry as to why he had disappeared: "I had to find out if I could have Christ without you Americans. I have discovered I can." His contempt for American efforts to bribe and threaten their way into influence in Iran made him determined to avoid involvement with us. He has. He continues to be a remarkable Christian working in a small city near Resht as director of an Iranian Red Cross hospital.

Frederick R. Wilson, Associate Coordinator,
Mission Program Services Unit, The United
Presbyterian Church U.S.A.,
Letter to Jeffrey C. Wood, April 1974.

1973. DAVID BURNIGHT

To the extent that we Christians are identified first of all with our nation-state, and only secondly with loyalty to the transcendent Lord who judges all nations, we have difficulty communicating our faith to persons who are critical of or who feel themselves oppressed by the action of our nation. They do not believe us. They see us as "culture-Christians." They reject our testimony to our Lord, because our real Lord seems to them to be the institution of our nation, or "anti-Communism" or "keeping America great" (at whatever cost to others of God's children). In the Biblical struggle with this transgression, it was called "idolatry." Contrariwise, to the extent that we put down these and other idolatries in the name of the Lord of all, we may be heard gratefully. Not all will join us, but opportunities for communicating our faith will be opened and multiplied. Just as important, our own faithfulness will be tested and deepened.

David Burnight, Statement to the 185th
General Assembly (1973), The United
Presbyterian Church U.S.A.

1972. A LITANY

God of Moses, saved in the river;

God of Israel, freed from Egypt, freed from the desert;

God of the slain Lamb, powerless Lion of Judah;

God of Brazil, of the millions exploited by the black magic of growth;

God of Mexico, of the ambivalence of the revolution;

God of New York, of disappointment and of new life;

God of the theologians, deceived by the wind of doctrine;

God of the bureaucrats, nervously searching for new programmes;

God of Africa, of a growing church in a land of exploitation;

God of the religious people, caught in the projection of their own mind;

God of the conservatives, of the burning desire to save souls;

God of the liberals, dreaming of reform;

God of the radicals, dreaming of revolution;

God of the artists, creativity of man;

God of the technocrats, enslaved to the power they hold;

God of the exploiters, love of power;

God of the Christians, between faith and unfaith;

God of those who have never heard of Jesus Christ;

God of those who have heard of Christ but only see his people;

God of us—God of all men,

surprise us anew with your faithfulness, save us today.   Bangkok Conference, 1972, World Council of
Churches. *International Review of Mission*,
Vol. 62 (April 1973).

Probing the Issues

—Assuming the accuracy of the *Ladies' Home Journal* survey, there are several points in it worth discussing: How true is it that we feel least hostile toward members of another religion? If love for Christ is measured by love for enemies, where may we locate major obstacles to that love?

—One measure of our comparative concern for aliens and citizens is provided by the local church budget. What priorities does your budget reflect in regard to concern for local, national, and worldwide causes? Dwindling support at home has forced every mission board to cut back its program: How does this fact reflect a widespread "Nazareth-syndrome" among us? To what degree does this bear out the judgments of Marty and Shaull?

—Let the group imagine that they are missionaries abroad who encounter the sort of problem Burnight and Wilson describe. How could they deal with this problem? By becoming citizens of the foreign country? By appealing to actions in which the U.S.A. churches have opposed our government? How can a representative of a "developed" country who is working in an "undeveloped" country avoid the charges of cultural imperialism or "dirty charity"?

—The substance of our prayers often indicates the range and force of our loves. Judging by the typical Sunday morning prayers in church, how well do we escape the "Nazareth-syndrome"? What should be done to extend the range of our concerns to embody the types mentioned in the Bangkok litany?

Reconsidering the Lucan Story of Nazareth

—Is it proper to read the Lucan account of Nazareth as if this were a parable of every town's response to the Gospel as well as the story of the first response?

—In the light of the group's discussions, what groups today provide the closest analogies to Luke's blind, poor, captives, the Sidonian widow, the Syrian leper? Did Luke have such analogies in mind?

—When we read this Scripture, what difference does it make whether we identify ourselves (and our congregation) with the blind or with the Sidonian widow, Elisha, the residents of Capernaum, or the people in Nazareth? Can Christians find within their own hearts some kinship with all of these? If so, does the story help us to come to terms with an inner struggle within each of us?

—When we become aware of how seriously American parochialisms compromise the power of the Christian mission today, we may ask on what grounds can we have confidence in the future of that mission? Does the Lucan story tend to strengthen or weaken that confidence?

—Is the God of the litany the same as the God of Jesus, of Elijah, of the men of Nazareth? If so, how does he save *all* of us? Is faith in this salvation what Christian faith is all about?

—After the people of Nazareth discovered that this liberation was not for them, what could they have done to reclaim that liberation?

Supplementary Reading

On the Scripture

Bornkamm, Günther, *Jesus of Nazareth* (London: Hodder & Stoughton, Ltd., 1960), pp. 75–82.

Jeremias, Joachim, *Jesus' Promise to the Nations* (London: SCM Press, Ltd., 1958).

Stoeger, A., *The Gospel According to St. Luke* (Herder & Herder, Inc., 1969), Vol. 1, pp. 82–88.

On the Voices

International Review of Mission, Vol. 62 (April, 1973).

Loew, Cornelius, *Modern Rivals to Christian Faith* (The Westminster Press, 1956).

Risk (World Council of Churches), Vol. 9, No. 3 (1973).

Salvation Today and Contemporary Experience: A Collection of Texts (World Council of Churches, 475 Riverside Drive, New York, N.Y. 10027).

On Civil Disobedience

The Scripture: I Peter 3:8–18; 4:12–19

(Consult the Revised Standard Version.)

The Discovery: A fiery ordeal is normal for Christians

In this letter a Christian elder wrote to several congregations that had run afoul of the law and were facing official trials, with possible penalties of death for some of their members. They had been ridiculed and slandered by pagan neighbors. Because of their loyalty to Christ, the martyr, they, too, were facing martyrdom, "a sprinkling with his blood" (1:2). Accused of many crimes, including that of "good behavior in Christ," they occasionally had the opportunity to give a defense of that behavior. Since the very name of Christ made them liable to conviction, they had to respond to "the law" in ways appropriate to that name. According to this letter, three sets of attitudes were required:

TOWARD legal adversaries and hostile public
    a. fearlessness, freedom from anxiety (3:14)

  b. innocence of such charges as theft and murder (4:15)

  c. readiness to be charged with "civil disobedience" (4:16)

  d. refusal to use evasions or deceit (3:10)

  e. the acceptance of unpopularity, ridicule, abuse (4:14)

  f. the return of good for evil, blessing instead of cursing (3:9)

  g. eagerness to give an account of their hope (3:15)

TOWARD fellow Christians

  a. readiness to suffer with them (3:8)

  b. unity of spirit and love (3:8)

  c. tender heart and humble mind (3:8)

  d. the strong pursuit of peace (3:11)

  e. the practice of hospitality (4:9)

  f. faithfulness in duties to the congregation (4:10)

TOWARD God

  a. acceptance of sufferings as his will (3:17; 4:17)

  b. sanity and soberness in prayers (4:7)

  c. reverence for Christ (3:15)

  d. complete trust in God's will (3:12, 17; 4:9)

  e. a clear conscience (3:16)

  f. joy (4:13)

  g. obedience to the gospel (4:17)

These three sets of attitudes were demanded by a situation in which loyalty to God had placed the church in conflict with loyalty to the laws, both religious and civil. In that situation Peter believed that Christ's example furnished an index to the kind of behavior which should be expected of all Christians. Christ had been executed as a lawbreaker; some of them faced the same execution, and under similar charges. Far from bemoaning such a fate, this author viewed it as an opportunity for rejoicing, and for glorifying God.

Some American Voices

Should Christians defy the law? Ever since New Testament days that question has provoked contrary answers within the church. Some have detected no need for it; others have believed it necessary if the church were to save its soul, to understand its gospel, and to be true to its vocation. This issue has divided many congregations.

1776. TIMOTHY DWIGHT

This continent is inhabited by a people who have the same religion, the same manners, the same interests, the same language, and the same essential forms and principles of civil government. This is an event which, since the building of Babel [Gen. 11:9] till the present time, the sun never saw. . . . The empire of North America will be the last on earth [and] . . . the most glorious. Here the progress of temporal things towards perfection will undoubtedly be finished. . . . Here will be accomplished that remarkable Jewish tradition that the last thousand years of the reign of time would, in imitation of the conclusion of the first week, become a glorious Sabbath of peace, purity, and felicity. . . . This continent will be the principal seat of that new, that peculiar kingdom, which shall be given to the saints of the Most High, . . . the greatest, the happiest of all dominions.

Timothy Dwight, Valedictory Address, Yale
College, July 25, 1776, in Winthrop S. Hudson
(ed.), Nationalism and Religion in America
(Harper & Row, Publishers, Inc., 1970),
pp. 59–61.

1935. H. RICHARD NIEBUHR

When faith loses its force, as generation follows generation, discipline is relaxed, repentance grows formal, corruption enters with idolatry, and the church, tied to the culture which it sponsored, suffers corruption with it. Only a new withdrawal followed by a new aggression can then save the church and restore to it the salt with which to savor society. . . . The task of the present generation appears to lie in the liberation of the church from its bondage to a corrupt civilization.

H. Richard Niebuhr, in H. Richard Niebuhr,
Wilhelm Pauck, and Francis P. Miller, The
Church Against the World (Willett, Clark &
Company, 1935), pp. 123, 124.

Good Friday, 1971. ROBERT MCAFEE BROWN

I am a citizen, a clergyman, a professor. I am also a father, and on this occasion I am proud to be blocking the entrance to this draft board in the company of my draft-age son. As a clergyman, I choose to preach my Good Friday sermon not in a church but on a pavement, not with words but with a deed. I am so grateful that today is not only

Good Friday but also the beginning of the feast of Passover, the time when Jews re-enact the liberation God gave his people.

The sermon I seek to do instead of say is very simple. It goes like this: "It is wrong for young men to go through these doors and be enrolled to kill. Since it is wrong it must be opposed. And we today are opposing it by blocking these doors in a spirit of nonviolent love."

Nonviolent love didn't work too well against the state that first Good Friday. The state won. Or so it seemed. But Easter turned the apparent defeat into victory; and showed that love can defeat fear and hate, that freedom is not finally held in bondage. At that point the message of Good Friday/Easter and the message of Passover are the same—love is conquering even when it seems to lose.

We, too, will seem to lose today. Once again the state will seem to win; we will be taken off to jail. But we affirm by our presence here that the power of love is stronger than the love of power, that no jail need imprison the human spirit, that Good Fridays can turn into Easters, that Passover triumphs can be repeated, and that as long as good men are being drafted to fight evil wars, we (or others like us) will return to this spot.

> A statement read in front of the Berkeley,
> California, draft board by Robert McAfee
> Brown prior to an act of civil disobedience.

1965. Louis Waldman

The open violation of the law is an open invitation to others to join in such violation. Disobedience to law is bad enough when done secretly, but it is far worse when done openly, especially when accompanied by clothing such acts in the mantle of virtue. . . . The secret violator recognizes his act for what it is: an antisocial act. . . . But the open violator, the agitating violator, acts shamelessly, in defiance of his neighbor's judgment.

> Louis Waldman, in Hugo A. Bedau (ed.), *Civil Disobedience: Theory and Practice* (Pegasus Books, The Bobbs-Merrill Company, Inc., 1969), p. 109.

1972. MORRIS I. LEIBMAN, JR.

Another major vice in the theory of civil disobedience is the terrible threat of zealotry and self-righteousness. This theory is inhumane, selfish, bigoted and arrogant. . . . This tactic generates hostility and heated emotions, it introduces a mob psychology into our politics, . . . produces a stress situation which no free society can long tolerate.

> Morris I. Leibman, Jr., in William S. Coffin and Morris I. Leibman, Jr., *Civil Disobedience: Aid or Hindrance to Justice* (Washington, D.C.: American Enterprise Institute for Public Policy Research, 1972).

1966. DANIEL BERRIGAN, S.J.

> Peacemaking is hard
> hard almost as war.
> The difference being one
> we can stake life upon
> and limb and thought and love.

I stake this poem out
dead man to a dead stick
to tempt an Easter chance—
if faith may be
truth, an evil chance
penultimate at last,

not last. We are not lost.

When these lines gathered
of no resource at all
serenity and strength,
it dawned on me—

a man stood on his nails

an ash like dew, a sweat
smelling of death and life.
Our evil Friday fled,
the blind face gently turned
another way, toward life

a man walks in his shroud

1971. WILLIAM SCHEICK

The Puritan's politics of religion has been transformed into the New Left's religion of politics.
. . . Tolerance, even neutrality, represents opposition to faith in their ideal. . . . They claim to bear

witness to some radical truth, to some ideal rooted in transcendental human needs. . . . They find it necessary to view the temporal world with suspicion, seeing themselves engaged in a movement of negation toward the existing world. . . . Both the Puritans and the New Left stress the importance and value of the private self; on the other hand, both equally tend to negate this sense of the self for a more collective goal. . . . [They] share this feeling that they are working for salvation while the earth is at the very verge of time. . . . The political-saint must be alert and he must act now in the immediacy of his present experience; his action may be violent or non-violent, but it must be militant. The New Left sees itself, as did the Puritans, as both the vanguard and the final force for life and truth at the close of history. For them time is short and the future is now.

William Scheick, in Martin E. Marty and Dean G. Peerman, *New Theology No. 9* (The Macmillan Company, 1972), pp. 107–117.

1963. KRISTER STENDAHL

The Sermon on the Mount is actually a rebellious manifesto which gives to disciples of Christ the right to break the Law in the name of Christ. But it is important to remember that it *is* subversive, and that the disciple must be prepared to pay the price for such action. . . . The license . . . can only be appropriated in faith, and will always threaten the equilibrium of God's created world.

Krister Stendahl, in Paul Peachey (ed.), *Biblical Realism Confronts the Nation* (Herald Press, 1963), p. 149.

1973. MARTIN LUTHER KING, JR.

My friends, I must say to you that we have not made a single gain in civil rights without determined legal and nonviolent pressure. . . .

We know through painful experience that freedom is never voluntarily given by the oppressor; it must be demanded by the oppressed. . . .

How does one determine whether a law is just or unjust? A just law is a man-made code that squares with the moral law or the law of God. An unjust law is a code that is out of harmony with the moral law. . . . Any law that uplifts human personality is just. Any law that degrades human personality is unjust. . . . I submit that an individual who breaks a law that conscience tells him is unjust, and who willingly accepts the penalty of imprisonment in order to arouse the conscience of the community over its injustice, is in reality expressing the highest respect for law.

> Martin Luther King, Jr., "Letter from
> Birmingham Jail," in *Why We Can't Wait*
> (Harper & Row, Publishers, Inc., 1963),
> pp. 82, 85, 86.

Probing the Issues

—What evidence can you cite to support Timothy Dwight's contention that the American government represents a fulfillment of the Biblical promises?

—Can the church be liberated in H. Richard Niebuhr's terms without entering into open conflict with the political and industrial and military rulers of present-day society?

—After reading thoughtfully the Sermon on the Mount (Matt., chs. 5 to 7), how would your group assess Stendahl's conclusions?

—Do you support Brown's understanding of how Good Friday and Easter should be celebrated by Christians? How many of us could join him in a similar celebration?

—In the light of Scheick's association of the New Left with the Puritans, does the group agree that radicals are as capable of nationalistic idolatry as are reactionaries? What are the most reliable marks of such idolatry?

—In reaction to Berrigan's verse, we may ask, Is it true that only those who are persecuted for their faith can fully grasp the gospel of death and resurrection, or be grasped by it?

—Evaluate, in Biblical and Christian terms, the merit in the arguments of Waldman, Leibman, and King.

Listening Again to I Peter

—Assuming that discussion has provoked a clash of opinions, how can we be helped to understand I Peter 3:8–9? What would be required to make it possible for Peter's readers to obey him?

—Having experienced among ourselves ways in which words can wound and make reconciliation more difficult, can we more fully appreciate Peter's emphasis on healing speech in 3:9–10, 15; 4:11, 16? Compare these teachings with Christ's Rules of Order (see Introduction).

—To what extent does *unity* of spirit require *uniformity* of attitude within the church, or does reverence for Christ encourage diversity? What limits did Peter set to such diversity?

—In what different ways and circumstances did Peter think Christians could be said to share in the sufferings of Christ? To what extent have those ways become obsolete today?

—If American churches were more faithful to the way of life of I Peter, would there be more or less civil disobedience? more or less persecution?

—Considering that the fiery ordeal may have endangered the very survival of the church, on what grounds could I Peter have such confidence in its triumph?

Supplementary Reading

On the Scripture

Hunter, Archibald M., and Homrighausen, Elmer G., "The First Epistle of Peter," *The Interpreter's Bible* (Abingdon Press, 1957), Vol. XII, pp. 124–141.

Moffatt, James, *The General Epistles* (Moffatt New Testament Commentary) (Harper & Brothers, 1928), pp. 135–143, 155–161.

On Civil Disobedience

Bedau, Hugo A. (ed.), *Civil Disobedience: Theory and Practice* (Pegasus Books, The Bobbs-Merrill Company, Inc., 1969).

Brown, Robert McAfee, *The Pseudonyms of God* (The Westminster Press, 1972).

Childress, James F., *Civil Disobedience and Political Obligation* (Yale University Press, 1971).

King, Martin Luther, Jr., "Letter from Birmingham Jail," *Why We Can't Wait* (Harper & Row, Publishers, Inc., 1963), pp. 77–100.

Lynd, Alice (ed.), *We Won't Go: Personal Accounts of War Objectors* (Beacon Press, Inc., 1968).

Songs of Pete Seeger.

Amnesty: Limited or Unlimited?

The Scripture: Luke 7:36–50

(Consult the Revised Standard Version or James Moffatt's translation.)

The Discovery: The righteous man is lost

Luke's story presents one version of an eternal triangle: two men and a woman. In this drama three actors appear, and a fourth stands invisible in the wings. Each of the visible players—Simon, the woman, Jesus—embodies a dominant force. The story sets up a collision among those forces. In the wings, as prompter and director, is the hidden God, the judge of sin and the source of forgiveness.

The woman expressed the impulse of penitence, for she acknowledged herself as a sinner and recognized in Jesus an offer of God's grace. Her weeping proved her penitence, and her care for Jesus proved how penitence is transformed into gratitude by forgiveness. Forgiven much, she loved much. In her, penitence plus gratitude equaled peace.

A different force moved Simon. He was honest

enough to call a spade a spade. He was outraged by Jesus' indifference to the woman's record. He felt he had no recourse but to condemn the woman and to attack Jesus. Yet Simon was the villain of the story. So powerful was his devotion to righteousness and honesty that no room was left in him for penitence or gratitude.

Jesus became the conduit for forgiveness, in its weakness and in its power. He saw into the hearts of the other two and gauged their sin and their love. He had been authorized by the hidden actor to cancel debts, whether small or large (v. 41). On this occasion God's forgiveness proved stronger than the woman's sin (she welcomed it), but weaker than Simon's (unable to overcome his resistance). Thus the story illustrates the relative power of those three forces—penitence, self-righteousness, forgiveness.

Yet we may venture to criticize the story on at least two grounds. In the first place, the identification of the actors prejudices the Christian reader. Simon is presented as a Pharisee—the kiss of death, for every reader knows that Pharisees are by definition villains and hypocrites. So, too, the reader will prejudge the woman sentimentally as a Christian in disguise. The same reader knows in advance that Jesus can say and do nothing wrong. The story is told to stifle dissent over Jesus' action.

In the second place, the story denies to the Pharisee the courtesy of "equal time"; he had no opportunity for rebuttal. Given the benefit of a free press, he could surely have mounted an impressive answer. As a sample:

> That crazy allegory put me in a trap, Lord. It does recognize the basic fact that the woman owes God a greater debt than I do, but it makes that fact the basis

for nonsense. What creditor would be stupid enough to cancel a debt of a thousand dinars as readily as one of a hundred? For God to do that would destroy his own Law and defy justice. It would invite everyone to break the greatest commands; it would deny justice to those who obey those commands, as well as to those who have been punished for their sins. This woman has defied the Ten Commandments. To ease her conscience by declaring her forgiven would make those commandments null and void. It would destroy respect for all law, and faith in all justice. You have been influenced by the sentimental show of affection and you have no firm evidence that God is as easy on such sinners as you are. Who are you to distort God's justice in this way?

Readers are invited to devise a parable that Simon might construct to correct the "insane" parable of Jesus. Undoubtedly Simon's substitute would be more in line with the theology of many Christians.

Some Contrary Voices

1974. LINDA CHARLTON

The involvement of American forces in the Vietnam war ended more than a year ago; but the complex, tangled and emotional question of amnesty for those who refused to fight in that war is still very much with the nation.

In three days of hearings last week by a subcommittee of the House Judiciary Committee, a parade of witnesses presented a mosaic of viewpoints. . . .

The Administration's position of absolute opposition to any type of amnesty for either draft evaders or deserters was matched by the equally forceful opposition of the pro-amnesty forces to anything less than a blanket and unconditional amnesty. In between were those like Senator Robert Taft, Jr., and former Secretary of the Army Robert F. Froehlke, who favored "conditional" amnesty at least for draft evaders. . . .

But it was apparent that the central question remained the moral one. The pro-amnesty forces, on the whole, seemed to be seeking not amnesty so much as vindication—certification by the granting of blanket amnesty to anyone involved in any way in Vietnam-protest activity, that the war was totally immoral, totally illegal. . . .

Fred E. Darling, an official of the Non-Commissioned Officers Association, had a different morality: To grant even conditional amnesty to these men, to "let them return to the country they have shunned" would be, he said, "a slap in the face to the millions of men who were drafted, who were wounded, who were maimed or who were killed in a bloody, unpopular war. . . . The good God calls upon us to be merciful—to forgive our trespassers —but he did not mention 'amnesty.'" . . .

The Pentagon . . . chose to avoid a direct assault on the thickets of morality and based its argument —against amnesty—on military pragmatism. In its official statement, the Pentagon eschewed "vengeance, vindictiveness, or retribution." But it maintained that amnesty for deserters would be bad for morale and discipline and "could establish a dangerous precedent" for any future draft.

And so the amnesty equation grows more com-

plex, with morality, legality, unacknowledged gut
reaction, precedent and pragmatic considerations
intertwined.

Linda Charlton, in *The New York Times*,
March 17, 1974.

1970. JEANETTE STRUCHEN

What's the point of forgiving everything, Lord?
Or have you stopped blushing like the rest of us?
  We wink at hanky-panky
        soft-pedal sin a-go-go
        tolerate crime
        perpetuate war
              and
        suspect peaceniks.
Why did you forgive the adulteress, Lord?
Was it a lesson teaching us to forgive
  anybody anything?
                    Or
  teaching us to accept the sinner
                        and
  condemn the sin?
That's complicated, Lord, and remember, some of us
  in the religious mod squad get confused by
  thinking.

From *Thank God for the Red, White and
Black,* by Jeanette Struchen. Copyright © 1970
by Jeanette Struchen. Reprinted by permission
of J. B. Lippincott Company.

1974. JEAN GATCH

I have been haunted by two phrases from Lincoln's Second Inaugural Address: "to bind up the
nation's wounds" and "to care for him who shall
have borne the battle." These are among the few

humane and hopeful sentiments that can come out of war.

Never in our history have we needed humanity and hope more than we need them now in the wake of the Vietnam disaster. It is time for amnesty for us all. . . .

Let us declare amnesty for all those political leaders who, misguided or not, led us to, and kept us in, Vietnam. Some were stupid, some heroic and some simple glory-mongers. But until we discover a wisdom machine to sort them into neat categories, we must rely on the only truth we do have: they are all Americans and all human. . . .

So it's time for amnesty for politicians, and for all of us who voted them in, failed to remove them, neglected to search out the facts, and simply turned the television knob to another channel. And for those of us who did protest and march and shout, but not always wisely or decently. And for those of us who maligned our congressmen for not risking the dangerous step of voting to stop money for the war but who continued to pay our taxes rather than risk the consequences of refusing. And for those of us who endured in silence the suspicion that the war went on partly because of the huge profits it meant to some but who never refused the wage hike or the dividends that profit made possible. . . .

It is certainly time for amnesty, in advance, for any odd, unkind, strange or excessive action or statement made by any war prisoner, his wife, any disfigured veteran or disillusioned Green Beret.

And it is certainly time to give total, no-holds-barred amnesty to all those who are in jail, in hiding, or in exile because they would not fight the war.

Surely there were men who went because they were cowards as well as cowards who refused to go. There were glory-mongers among the hawks, as well as among the doves. And there were surely heroes in both camps. . . .

But amnesty does not mean forgetfulness. Please God, we must remember it all—remember it and study it and learn from it. . . .

There is guilt enough for us all. There must also be amnesty for us all.

> Jean Gatch, in *The New York Times*,
> January 12, 1974.

1974. WILLIAM S. WHITE

The pro-amnesty lobby is having a field day in hurling around great blobs of mawkish sentimentality. Draft dodging and even desertion in the face of the enemy ought to be "forgiven" and in some cases even rewarded.

The deserters and evaders themselves are availing themselves, from their refuge in Canada, of the American TV tube to appeal to the qualities of compassion and forgiveness.

But not all of them are stopping there. Some are "demanding that their admitted violations of criminal law be redefined as acts of a higher law and a higher morality." They declare their willingness to come home only if the United States apologizes to them.

For them not even proposals to let them work off their refusal to accept the common duty and the common dangers of their generation by various forms of vague do-goodism are enough. . . .

It is therefore difficult to determine which side of this nonsense is more insulting to the young Americans who did the fighting and dying. Which group is more insolent?

Is it the politicians who offer this so-called method of atonement? Or is it the arrogant group of those who wish almost to be canonized for having let some other youngster carry the rifle through the sinks of Vietnam?

. . . What happens to the security of this country and to the armed services themselves if every young man is to be allowed to serve or not serve as he may choose, pleading a special sensitivity and a special morality? . . .

The anti-amnesty people are not motivated by "revenge." They see instead fairness in sacrifice, the security of a nation and equal—not unequal— justice under the law.

William S. White, in *The Journal-Courier,* New
Haven, Connecticut, March 21, 1974.

1969. UNITED CHURCH OF CHRIST

In the interests of reconciliation and the binding up of wounds, for the sake of our freedoms and to allow our high respect for conscience, in the best tradition of a strong and secure democracy, in the name of Christian love, we urge the President of the United States to grant, at the earliest possible opportunity, amnesty and pardon for those who for actions witnessing to their beliefs have been incarcerated, deprived of their rights of citizenship, or

led by their conscience into exile during the course
of the nation's great agony in the Vietnam war. We
urge these bold actions because this nation needs,
and is strong enough to embrace, both those who
have engaged in the Vietnam conflict and those
who have opposed it.

United Church of Christ, Seventh General
Synod, June 25 to July 2, 1969, Boston,
Massachusetts.

1974. COALITION OF WAR RESISTERS

As people who have been opposed to the United
States Government's war in Indochina and face
prison or other loss of rights because of our opposition, we demand universal, unconditional amnesty. This does not mean forgiveness or forgetfulness for our acts of resistance of which we are
proud. Nor does it mean that we are begging permission to "return to the fold." We are calling on
the American people to demand with us that the
U.S. Government stop any efforts to prosecute us
or deny our rights because of our just acts of resistance.

Specifically, we demand immediate amnesty
without conditions (such as alternative service) and
without case-by-case review, for:

—all military resisters (including "deserters")
and draft resisters, whether in exile or underground in the U.S.;

—all persons who, because of their opposition to
the war and the military, have been adminis-
tratively punished, convicted by civilian or
military courts, or are subject to prosecution;

—all veterans with less-than-honorable discharges. . . .

Some of us are in exile; some of us have made
permanent homes outside the U.S.; most people
who need amnesty are in the U.S. Some of us do or
will need to surface from underground, return
from exile, or fight for individual upgrading of
less-than-honorable discharges. But wherever we
live, and wherever we see our future, we are one
in the conviction that it was right to resist participation in the U.S. Government's war in Indochina.
This is what we mean by amnesty.

Coalition of American War Resisters in Canada,
Vancouver, B.C., December 13, 1973.

Probing the Issues

An individual can base his attitude toward the problem of amnesty either on general grounds or on Christian grounds. The discussion *within the church* gives an
opportunity for each person to distinguish between political and religious considerations. It may be an important objective for the group to learn how to make that
distinction and how to hold to it. Once that distinction
is clear, a person may find that his opposition to
amnesty in this situation is based on Christian grounds,
or that his support is based on secular considerations,
e.g., Gatch makes no explicit appeal to Christian faith;
that White could make such an appeal is conceivable.
The basic problem for the church is how to bring its
distinctive faith to bear on this political issue.

—For many the question of amnesty raises the prior
question of whether this war, or any war of this

kind, can be justified on moral or Christian grounds. The group's discussion of this prior question may well absorb all of the time.

—In response to the voice of Jean Gatch, we may ask, Wherein lie the reasons why people oppose amnesty for all? Is it easier or harder for veterans to grant amnesty to deserters than for C.O.'s to grant "amnesty" to the hawks among wartime politicians?

—Most participants will agree that the church has a vocation separate from that of the nation. It has a mission to each individual, to alienated groups, whether young or old, to the people who will be asked to fight in future wars, to other nations besides America. How do its various attitudes toward amnesty contribute to its vocation with regard to these various constituencies?

—Assume that a returning deserter, liable to arrest and criminal punishment, should appeal to your family or congregation to provide a secret sanctuary for three weeks until he can move on to another station on the "underground railway." How would you respond, and why?

Ruling out both amnesty and revenge, President Gerald Ford, in August 1974, declared himself in favor of offering an "earned reentry" into the national community for war resisters and deserters. What conditions for such reentry do you think are fair? How has the President's program of "conditional amnesty" worked out? For the deserters and draft dodgers? For the dishonorably discharged? What further steps does your group recommend?

Listening Again to Luke

—Many participants deny any connection between amnesty (forgetfulness) and forgiveness, and thereby deny any applicability of Luke, ch. 7, to the current issue. Potential recipients of amnesty say that to accept forgiveness would require them to confess that they had done wrong; potential donors claim that in denying amnesty they do not deny the Christian obligation to forgive. Evaluate the truth involved in this distinction between amnesty and forgiveness. Should either party, as a Christian, deny a share in wrongdoing, and therefore the need for forgiveness? How is forgetting linked to forgiving? In what sense could Jesus' action be called God's declaration of amnesty? To what degree can personal attitudes be separated from legal acts?

—The current discussion on amnesty may disclose the fact that Jesus' position in Luke, ch. 7, was by no means a simple one. Did his act of grace require a difficult act of humiliation by *both* the woman and Simon? Did his action toward one person involve injustice toward others? Should persons never determine their own readiness to forgive by the relative degrees of merit on the part of those to be forgiven? Did Jesus ignore the difficulties of translating merciful attitudes on the part of individuals into legal policies established by religious and political institutions?

—Those who fear amnesty often fear the effects that it will have on social institutions. Does this fear help us to understand why Jesus' practice of unlimited forgiveness released such explosive hostility? Should any secular government be expected to determine its policies by reference to God's way of governing mankind?

—The Gospel tradition speaks with one voice in demanding that every disciple forgive others. Does our confession that Jesus is Lord become an outright lie if we disobey that demand?

Supplementary Reading

On the Scripture

Jeremias, Joachim, *Parables of Jesus* (Charles Scribner's Sons, 1962), pp. 124–136.

Kierkegaard, Søren, *Christian Discourses* (Oxford University Press, 1939), pp. 379–386.

Knox, John, "The Gospel According to St. Luke," *The Interpreter's Bible* (Abingdon Press, 1952), Vol. VIII, pp. 141–146.

Stoeger, A., *The Gospel According to St. Luke* (Herder & Herder, Inc., 1969), Vol. 1, pp. 141–146.

On Amnesty

Amnesty Education Packet. National Interreligious Board for Conscientious Objectors, 550 Washington Building, 15th Street and New York Avenue., N.W., Washington, D.C. 20005.

Amnesty Packet. American Civil Liberties Union, 22 East 40th Street, New York, N.Y. 10016. Also available: a one-hour videotape of debate between William F. Buckley and Henry Schwarzchild and a one-hour tape cassette.

Film: *Duty Bound.* Broadcasting and Film Division, National Council of Churches, 475 Riverside Drive, New York, N.Y. 10027.

Further information on problems still confronting deserters, draft resisters, and the less honorably discharged is available from Special Ministries/Vietnam Generation, National Council of Churches, Room 766, 475 Riverside Drive, New York, N.Y. 10027.

The above references may be updated by consulting articles in recent journals as indexed in the *Readers' Guide to Periodical Literature* under Amnesty.

On Ending Segregation

The Scripture: Colossians 3:1–11

(Consult the Revised Standard Version or the New American Bible.)

The Discovery: You have died

Usually when we read a passage, we follow the movement of thought step by step from the beginning. After we have read this passage, let us reverse the process, beginning at the end and working backward. Starting with Paul's conclusion we will trace the four steps that led him to that conclusion.

Step 1: v. 11. Eight types of people are mentioned; these eight form the sharpest ravines in society known to the author. One person is separated from others by nation, race, religion, status, education. These are among the most rigid barriers in human society, boundaries fortified by custom, prejudice, law, wealth, and military power. No society in human history has been free of them. The author includes them all in order to announce the end of them all, in order to stress the opening words: "Here there cannot be. . . ." *Here* refers to a community already in existence. In that community owners and slaves live as equals, as do men and women from both sides of the other barricades. Incredible! Miraculous! Has any of us ever stood at such a place? Probably not. And yet the author says *yes*. What can he mean? For an answer we must retrace the path of his thinking.

Step 2: vs. 9–10. The chasms that separate the eight groups have been overcome only because they have all been located within two more inclusive societies. To one society all eight belong, with all their accumulated antipathies and antagonisms. To another society they do not belong. What language is adequate to cover such vast territory? The language of two *natures,* two *creations,* two *humanities,* two *Adams.* The conflicts among the eight groups have arisen *there* and *then* in an old society; they have become obsolete *here* and *now* in a new society. The practices of the old humanity were all adapted to its built-in antagonisms; the practices of the new humanity exhibit its "perfect harmony" (v. 14). Here and now creation is continuing, and society is being renewed "after the image of its creator." Now that it is possible to be included in this *here* and *now* society, how badly do we really want to belong to it?

Step 3: vs. 5–8. The answer may be this: when we see that we must migrate from the old society to the new, we may lose our eagerness. Our egos may well prefer the old ordering of things, an ordering where primary loyalties have become nailed to a particular race or nation or class or religion. Even though endless civil war is the price of those loyalties, we may still prefer to pay that price. After all, our pride, our security, our honor are invested in that society. To renounce it would be a form of suicide. Nevertheless, this author makes clear the result of that choice: to live in a society dominated by those loyalties is a sure way to pollute creation itself with idolatry, fornication, greed. The "old" man assumes that *in*-group loyalties are good, ignoring the fact that every such loyalty, by excluding some *out*-group, encourages the use of anger and malice and deceit toward them. Every member of that *out*-group becomes a potential enemy. The entrance to the new society is the suicide of the ego which lives by these loyalties and antagonisms. The choice is a choice of death (v. 5).

Step 4: vs. 1–4. And yet the congregation addressed in this letter has already made that choice. "You have died . . . you have been raised . . . your life is hid with Christ . . . you have put on the new nature." Transition from the old to the new society has already been made —at the cost of dying with Christ, at the cost of Christ's death.

Here is a boundary more decisive than any barricade among men—death and resurrection. The divisions in the old society cease to apply to dead men. None of those walls go as deep as *this* grave or rise as high as *this* heaven. You have died. When was that? Good Friday; his death included yours. His death turned your walls into doors. His death and his life are the death and life of the new society. "Here there cannot be. . . ." Do we find divisions in our congregation? Yes. Do we find them in Christ? No. If this be so, can our congregation claim Christ as "our life"? Not without putting an end to every form of segregation within itself, at the cost of dying. "You have died. . . . Put to death therefore." These two signs mark the boundary of the church. We find the church *only* where people, having once crossed this boundary, obey that command every day.

Some Contemporary Voices

Racism has been a perennial problem within the church. The Letter of Paul to the Colossians reflects its presence in ancient Colossae, just as every newspaper discloses its presence in our churches. The following voices plunge us into the vortex of perplexities and stimulate discussion simultaneously with the world and with the Bible.

1973. A CONFERENCE OF AMERICAN EVANGELICALS

We acknowledge that God requires justice. But we have not proclaimed or demonstrated his justice to an unjust American society. Although The Lord calls us to defend the social and economic rights of the poor and the oppressed, we have mostly remained silent. We deplore the historic involvement of the church in America with racism and the conspicuous responsibility of the evangelical community for perpetuating the personal attitudes and institutional structures that have divided the body of Christ along color lines. Further, we have failed to condemn the exploitation of racism at home and abroad by our economic system.

We affirm that God abounds in mercy and that he forgives all who repent and turn from their sins. So we call our fellow evangelical Christians to demonstrate repentance in a Christian discipleship that

confronts the social and political injustice of our
nation.

A Declaration of Evangelical Social Concern,
November 25, 1973, Chicago.

1970. JAMES BALDWIN

The American triumph—in which the American
tragedy has always been implicit—was to make
black people despise themselves. When I was little
I despised myself. I did not know any better. And
this meant, albeit unconsciously, or against my will,
or in great pain, that I also despised my father. *And*
my mother. *And* my brothers. *And* my sisters.
Black people were killing each other every Saturday night out on Lenox Avenue, when I was growing up: and no one explained to them, or to me,
that it was *intended* that they should: that they
were penned where they were, like animals, in
order that they should consider themselves no better than animals. Everything supported this sense
of reality, nothing denied it: and so one was ready,
when it came to go to work, to be treated as a slave.
So one was ready, when human terrors came, to
bow before a white God and beg Jesus for salvation
—this same white God who was unable to raise a
finger to do so little as to help you pay your rent,
unable to be awakened in time to help you save
your child.

There is always, of course, more to any picture
than can speedily be perceived, and in all of this—
groaning and moaning, watching, calculating,
clowning, surviving and outwitting—some tre-
mendous strength was nevertheless being forged

which is part of our legacy today. But that particular aspect of our journey now begins to be behind us. The secret is out: we are men.

But the blunt, open articulation of this secret has frightened the nation to death. I wish I could say "to life," but that is much to demand of a disparate collection of displaced people still cowering in their wagon trains and singing "Onward Christian Soldiers." The nation, *if* America is a nation, is not in the least prepared for this day. It is a day which the Americans never expected or desired to see, however piously they may declare their belief in "progress and democracy." Those words, now, on American lips, have become a kind of universal obscenity; for this most unhappy people, strong believers in arithmetic, never expected to be confronted with the algebra of their history.

Excerpts from an open letter from James Baldwin to Angela Davis, November 19, 1970, in *Risk*, Vol. 9, No. 3 (1973), pp. 73–74.

1974. JAMES H. CONE

Twentieth-century white theologians are still secure in their assumption that important theological issues emerge, primarily if not exclusively, out of the white experience. Despite the sit-ins and pray-ins, the civil rights movement and Black Power, Martin Luther King and Stokely Carmichael, white theologians still continue their business as usual. These theologians fail to realize that such a procedure is just as racist and oppressive against black people as Billy Graham's White House sermons. This is so because the black judgment on this mat-

ter is that those who are not for us must be against
us.

. . . If one takes seriously the exploitation and
suffering of black people in America and Jesus'
proclamation that he came "to set at liberty those
who are oppressed" (Luke 4:18), then the absence
of the urgency of the gospel of black liberation in
modern and contemporary American theology can
only confirm Marx's contention that "your very
ideas are but the outgrowth of the conditions of
your bourgeois production and bourgeois property."

> James H. Cone, Address to the American
> Theological Society, April 19, 1974.

1974. FRANK LOGUE

Zoning is a religion in the American suburb, a
faith that shapes hillsides, if it does not move mountains. Challenges to that faith, such as a proposal to
amend the regulations in a one-house-per-acre
zone to permit the construction of apartments,
give rise to such affirmations as: "One acre zoning
is the rock upon which I built my house." The
serious proponent of social change does not lightly
disregard such strongly held beliefs. Those who
would question as I do the present uses of suburban
zoning would do well to acknowledge the affirma-
tive values of the way of life which it both reflects
and sustains. . . .

Even honestly administered zoning regulations
. . . may contribute directly to the most serious
division in American life: the physical, social, educational, cultural and political separation of the ur-

ban poor—many of whom are black or Spanish-speaking—from the suburban middle class, nearly all of whom are white.

Frank Logue, in Connecticut Civil Liberties
Union *News*, April 1974.

1974. GARY L. CHAMBERLAIN

While 91 per cent of the Catholics and Protestants interviewed in a recent survey agreed that "Love thy neighbor" means that all races should be treated alike and that blacks should have the same rights and opportunities as others, 40 per cent said they would move if several black families came to live on their block, and 33 per cent indicated that they did not want blacks in their churches.

Gary L. Chamberlain, "Has 'Benign Neglect'
Invaded the Churches?" in *The Christian
Century,* April 24, 1974, p. 451.

1958. EVERETT TILSON

Certainly this biblical doctrine raises serious questions for those Christians among us with a desire for the preservation of segregation. God receives us into fellowship with himself on the sole condition of our grateful acceptance of his prodigal generosity. This being so, how dare we insist on additional prerequisites for the joint participation of other men with us in a branch of this fellowship? If God ignores such qualifying factors as sex, race and nationality in his gracious offer of forgiveness, can we make a legitimate claim to membership in the fellowship of the forgiven if we respect such factors? . . .

And it raises questions of no less significance for those Christians among us in favor of integration. For if we look on our emancipation from race prejudice as proof of superior virtue, do we not thereby deny the doctrine of salvation by grace? And if God's forgiveness knows no limit, can we lightly and indiscriminately dismiss all segregationalists as expendables in the holy war for first-class citizenship for all our people?

. . . While the Bible provides considerable support for both the theory and the practice of integration—at least of the members of the people of God—this fact must not be viewed as a ground for boasting. God is our redeemer, and not we ourselves.

Everett Tilson, Segregation and the Bible
(Abingdon Press, 1958), pp. 105, 106.

1972. BANGKOK CONFERENCE

It was the drug scene, you were lost and wretched, and you put your hand in the hand of the man who calmed the sea.

      I rejoice with you, my sister.

You are turned on by the exciting and ever-deepening insights of Scripture.

      I rejoice with you, my brother.

You were converted from shallowness to mystic depths through discipline and meditation.

      I rejoice with you, my sister.

You were a poor Mexican baptized by the Holy Spirit and the Blood of the Lamb.

      I rejoice with you, my brother.

You were an intellectual Chinese who broke

through the barrier between yourself and the
dung-smelling peasant.

I rejoice with you, my sister.
You found all the traditional language meaningless
and became "an atheist by the grace of God."

I rejoice with you, my brother.
Out of the depths of your despair and bondage you
cried and in your cry was poignant hope.

I rejoice with you, my sister.
You were oppressed and put down by male authority and in spite of sneers and snarls persevered in
your quest for dignity.

I rejoice with you, my sister.
For all my brothers and sisters who have entered
the struggle for social and spiritual liberation—I
rejoice.

Victory and grace be unto you.

Bangkok Conference, 1972, World Council of
Churches. *International Review of Mission*,
Vol. 62 (April 1973), pp. 196–197.

1926. THE IMPERIAL WIZARD OF THE KU KLUX KLAN

There are three of these great racial instincts,
vital elements in both the historic and the present
attempts to build an America which shall fulfill the
aspirations and justify the heroism of the men who
made the nation. These are the instincts of loyalty
to the white race, to the traditions of America, and
to the spirit of Protestantism, which has been an
essential part of Americanism ever since the days
of Roanoke and Plymouth Rock. They are con-

densed into Klan slogan: "Native, white, Protestant
supremacy."

The Imperial Wizard of the Ku Klux Klan,
quoted in Robert T. Handy, *A Christian
America* (Oxford University Press, 1971), p. 199.

1974. WILL D. CAMPBELL

I know how easy . . . it is to identify with the most
obvious minority—in this case the Blacks—and dismiss a less obvious minority—the rednecks, wool-
hats, peckerwoods, po' whites—as "the Enemy."
But there is a real sense in which the redneck has
been victimized beyond the Black. . . . He, too,
historically was a slave—a more sneaky kind of
slavery. . . . The redneck, not the Black, has been
the unseen factor . . . when it comes to the solution
of what seems to be our most pressing social problem: poverty/race/war. Moreover he has been
used by us all as a whipping post.

Will D. Campbell, in *Katallagete*, Spring 1974,
pp. 34 f.

Probing the Issues

—What arguments compatible with Christian faith
can be mounted in support of existing segregation
patterns among Christians? For example, Many
black Christians now reject integrated churches
because they would be dominated by the white
majorities. Is this racism in reverse? How does it
accord with Col., ch. 3?

—What losses are sustained by a congregation whose
membership is limited to a single race or class or

cultural group? How is its mission, whether domestic or foreign, affected by this same limitation? What changes of attitude are necessary before your own congregation can experience the joy of the Bangkok litany?

—We frequently hear the charge that the Christian church is the most segregated institution in American society. Let us analyze our own congregation in its surroundings in order to measure the truth of that charge. Which groups feel at home and which do not? Are there hidden barriers to membership? If so, where are they located?

—How do the churches in town encourage or oppose the various governmental agencies that seek to erase segregation? The zoning commission, urban redevelopment committees, recreational organizations, busing to schools? In what ways do the churches use their political clout to resist the extension of civil rights?

—At what points in the area does racial segregation coincide with types of employment, with school enrollments, with housing restrictions, with participation in cultural activities, with church membership?

—In what activities do these political, economic, and cultural conflicts come to the surface within the life of the parish? Are they more or less acute within the church than within the schools, the chamber of commerce, or the political parties?

**Looking Again at the Scripture's Picture
of the Church**

—Why and how did the death of Jesus effectively
introduce a new humanity into existence? In what
respects have the intervening centuries changed
the character of that humanity?

—Do you visualize the Colossian church as basically
different from churches in Columbus or Pittsfield?
If so, which differences might justify the practice of
segregation today?

—To bring Col. 3:11 up-to-date and make it applicable to your community, what groups would you
substitute for Greek, Jew, etc.?

—Next Sunday morning look over the worshiping
congregation. Then read Col. 3:1–11. Is there any
similarity between the two pictures? Does the contrast make you laugh, or cry, or what?

—How fully does the citation from Bangkok reflect
the same attitudes as the Colossian letter?

—Suppose that we cannot honestly apply Col. 3:11 to
our own congregation. How, then, do we explain
this if we hold to the logic of Colossians? Did
Christ's death not have enough power to destroy
these barriers? Have we neither died nor been
raised with Christ? Is there some other option?

—To what extent do we discover here another reason
why Jesus was crucified and his followers in the first

century persecuted? Is his death, then, the only force that can bring men to their senses, and show them the cost of their own prejudices?

Supplementary Reading

On Colossians

Beare, Francis W., and MacLeod, G. Preston, "The Epistle to the Colossians," *The Interpreter's Bible* (Abingdon Press, 1955), Vol. XI, pp. 207–208.

Carson, Herbert M., *Epistles of Paul to the Colossians and to Philemon* (Tyndale Bible Commentaries) (Wm. B. Eerdmans Publishing Company, 1960), pp. 79–86.

Hunter, Archibald M., *Galatians—Colossians* (Layman's Bible Commentary) (John Knox Press, 1959), Vol. 22, pp. 135–139.

On Segregation

Coles, Robert, *Children of Crisis*, Vol. 2: *Migrants, Mountaineers, and Sharecroppers* (Little, Brown & Company, 1972).

Cone, James H., *A Black Theology of Liberation* (J. B. Lippincott Company, 1970).

Herzog, Frederick, *Liberation Theology* (The Seabury Press, Inc., 1972).

Kelsey, George D., *Racism and the Christian Understanding of Man* (Charles Scribner's Sons, 1965).

Tilson, Everett, *Segregation and the Bible* (Abingdon Press, 1958).

Rich Nations, Poor Nations

The Scripture: James 2:1–13

(Consult the Revised Standard Version or the New English Bible.)

The Discovery: Partiality for the rich is murder

Digging in an ancient rubbish heap, an archaeologist can recover a few jagged pieces of pottery, piece them together until the entire jug takes its original shape. From this he can identify the period when it was baked in the kiln, and describe the culture of that period and place. So, too, the literary archaeologist, by studying a few sentences in an ancient manuscript, can recover many features of the author's way of thinking and living. One such feature in this passage is a basic contrast between two "spaces" in which people can live. The author calls these spaces *the world* and *the kingdom.* He addresses a group of brothers who in *the world* are poor but who are heirs of *the kingdom.* These two spaces are characterized by contradictory sets of convictions:

The world is that living space where

persons draw distinctions among themselves, setting themselves up as judges of their competitors. (V. 4.)

one distinction of high importance is a person's wealth. (V. 3.)

the value of an individual's jewelry and clothing determines the honor he can claim from those who are poorer. (V. 2.)

a person can use the courts to his advantage, increasing his own wealth and the poor man's poverty. (V. 6.)

an individual can use the laws and his own wealth as instruments of oppression. (V. 6.)

the system is so rigged as to show little mercy to the weak. (V. 13.)

some moral rules may be observed, yet murder continues to be done with impunity. (V. 11.)

the rule of law may be recognized, but not the law of liberty, which is the same law as the love of neighbor. (Vs. 8, 12.)

The kingdom is that living space where

the measure of glory and nobility is provided by Jesus. (V. 1.)

God has confounded the usual measurements of wealth by making the poor rich. (V. 5.)

those who love God and their neighbor become heirs of this realm. (Vs. 5, 8.)

the inhabitants have received God's name, proof of belonging to him and sharing in his honor. (V. 7.)

persons refuse to dishonor God's work by showing favoritism for the rich. (Vs. 1, 9.)

in the residents' treatment of one another, as in God's

treatment of them, mercy is more powerful than justice. (V. 13.)

for these residents, public morality is as important as private morality. (V. 11.)

the inhabitants judge themselves constantly by the law of the kingdom, the law of love, the law of liberty. (Vs. 8, 12.)

There is one map for the world and another for the kingdom; and yet both realms, in spite of the warfare between them, have met within the Christian assembly. As Christian men and women come together to worship God and to hail Jesus as "Lord of glory," the world is caught invading the kingdom. One clear sign of invasion is detected in the instinctive gesture of respect accorded to the better dressed members. That action belongs to the world and not to the kingdom; therefore it merits the charge of lawlessness, blasphemy, and even murder. On the map of the world, wealth gives to the wealthy a status that conceals the guilt in such action; the map of the kingdom makes that guilt highly visible.

Contemporary Voices

The objective reader of the New Testament must reckon with Jesus' forthright condemnations of the wealthy (e.g., Luke 6:24–26). Yet American Christians belong to the wealthiest nation on earth. Profiting daily from that wealth, they listen daily to news of "absolute poverty" in many other nations. Such wealth and such news make them vulnerable to the accusations of James, that is, if the law of which James spoke is still in force. Does that law in fact apply to wealthy nations?

1974. KURT WALDHEIM

The main theme of the Assembly is to secure the optimum use of the world's natural resources with the basic objective of securing better conditions of social justice throughout the world. Let me suggest six primary issues which demand immediate action if progress is to be made in achieving that objective.

First, mass poverty. The single most devastating indictment of our current world civilization is the continued existence of stark, pervasive mass poverty among two-thirds of the world population. It permeates every phase of life in developing countries: in the malnutrition of children, in the outbreaks of diseases, in widespread unemployment, in low literacy rates, in overcrowded cities. . . .

Second, the population of the world. It is anticipated that this special session will meet for three weeks. In that time the number of human beings on this planet will increase by four million. The increasing population of the world presents a constantly growing demand on our limited natural resources.

Third, food. Never in recent decades have world reserves been so frighteningly low. The production of enough food to feed, even reasonably well, people all over the world—let alone to transport and distribute it—almost certainly represents the largest single pressure on our natural resources.

Fourth, energy. The world at large has suddenly realized the critical importance of energy in our daily lives. The natural resources which provide the world's energy represent one of our most valuable heritages.

Fifth, military expenditure. During the three weeks of this Assembly session some $14 billion will have been spent on armaments. This enormous expenditure by itself represents yet another vast pressure on our natural resources.

Sixth, the world monetary system. An effective world monetary system is essential if our natural resources are to be used to the best advantage. The existing system is not working efficiently. It contains a most dangerous, cancer-like disease—inflation.

Each of these problems—all directly related to our natural resources—has a direct bearing on the future peace and stability of the world. No member state can insulate itself from their effects.

Kurt Waldheim, Address at United Nations,
Special Session of the General Assembly,
April 9, 1974.

1974. ANTHONY LEWIS

In one short sentence recently Professor Jean Mayer of Harvard, the great nutritionist, illuminated the profound moral and political test that awaits this country on the issue of food. "The same amount of food that is feeding 210 million Americans," he said, "would feed 1.5 billion Chinese on an average Chinese diet."

The question is: Will we, can we, go on pursuing our extravagant way of life in an increasingly hungry world? It is not some remote or speculative question. Half the people in the world now go to bed hungry every night. And the looming probability is that thousands, even millions, may starve in the year ahead unless they get help from outside—mainly from the U.S. . . .

And so we Americans shall probably have to decide before the end of 1974: Do we avert our gaze from Asia, cut ourselves adrift from a main problem of mankind? Or do we help others survive by doing the food equivalent of turning down our thermostats? . . . We can help on the scale needed only by adjusting our own eating habits.

Anthony Lewis, in The New York Times,
April 22, 1974.

1974. Richard L. Strout

The so-called poverty line in India . . . is an income of $30 a year, and 30% of the population (175 million people) live below it. . . . India needs fertilizer. The price has tripled. It needs oil to run irrigation pumps. The price has quadrupled. It needs about 108 million tons of grain a year to avert famine, but this depends on the weather or the reluctant generosity of patrons like the U.S. and U.S.S.R.

Richard L. Strout, in
The Christian Science Monitor, May 17, 1974.

1974. Hubert H. Humphrey

A fundamental moral choice cannot be evaded. Can a nation whose nutritionists proclaim obesity to be a leading health problem share its bountiful food resources with those whose very survival is at stake? . . . A decision by Americans to eat one less hamburger a week would make some 10 million tons of grain available for food assistance.

> Hubert H. Humphrey, Address, Rensselaer
> Meeting, United Nations, May 9, 1974.

1974. REPRESENTATIVE OF THE NETHERLANDS

Development efforts have failed to change the structural relationship of inequality and dependence between the poor and the rich nations. . . . This state of affairs cannot continue. We cannot accept this injustice of persistent backwardness with its grave hidden tensions and its threat to world peace.

> Speech delivered at Special Session of General
> Assembly of the United Nations, April, 1974.

The following five quotations are drawn from speeches in the U.S. House of Representatives, on January 23, 1974, opposing legislation to provide funds for International Development Assistance by way of long-term loans through the World Bank.

1974. WAYNE L. HAYS, Ohio Congressman

We can talk about what we ought to do for the poor of the world and all that, but what this is going to be is another subsidy for Kuwait and Saudi Arabia and the rest of the oil producing nations who are striking not only our nation but also mangling the poor of the underdeveloped nations of the world.

> Excerpt from debate in Congress,
> January 23, 1974.

1974. H. R. GROSS, Iowa Congressman

I am opposed to the gouging out of the pockets of the people of this country or using the printing presses of the Treasury to print another $1.5 billion to be broadcast to the four winds in foreign countries.

Excerpt from debate in Congress,
January 23, 1974.

1974. TIM LEE CARTER, Kentucky Congressman

We really have not seen visible effects of this (program) except that we have lost billions of dollars. We do not even retain the friendship of many of these countries, and in the United Nations they vote against us.

Excerpt from debate in Congress,
January 23, 1974.

1974. JOHN H. DENT, Pennsylvania Congressman

If tomorrow the producing countries decided not to send us any chrome, . . . this country would come to a standstill in 90 days. Giving this aid to these countries without some kind of string attached puts us in the position of being suckers.

Excerpt from debate in Congress,
January 23, 1974.

1974. BILL D. BURLISON, Missouri Congressman

I hope the House today will make known in no uncertain terms that America is ready to start taking care of the problems in this country, and will not continue to provide support for the rest of the world.

Excerpt from debate in Congress,
January 23, 1974.

1974. CONSULTATION ON GLOBAL JUSTICE

As Americans, we have come to realize how many of our national policies, of our institutional structures of production, marketing and defense, and of our current personal patterns of conduct and consumption, are all inextricably linked to the ongoing and explosive global catastrophe of famine, hunger and malnutrition which continues to claim millions of lives every year.... Our religious convictions compel us to take a stand on the side of the poor, the powerless and the oppressed. This means, in effect, a commitment not merely to bring immediate relief to the suffering, but also to work toward the creation of global structures which will ensure basic dignity and humane existence for all people.

Aspen, Colorado, Consultation on Global
Justice, in *The New York Times*, June 8, 1974.

1973. ROBERT S. MCNAMARA

Absolute poverty is a condition of life so degraded by disease, illiteracy, malnutrition and squalor as to deny its victims basic human necessities. It is a condition of life suffered by relatively few in the developed nations but by hundreds of millions of the citizens of the developing countries:

—One-third to one-half of the two billion human

beings in those countries suffer from hunger or malnutrition.

—20% to 25% of their children die before their fifth birthdays. And millions of those who do not die lead impeded lives because their brains have been damaged, their bodies stunted and their vitality sapped by nutritional deficiencies.

—The life expectancy of the average person is 20 years less than in the affluent world. They are denied 30% of the lives those of us from the developed nations enjoy. In effect, they are condemned at birth to an early death.

—800 million of them are illiterate and, despite the continuing expansion of education in the years ahead, even more of their children are likely to be so.

> Robert S. McNamara, Address to the Board of
> Governors of the World Bank,
> September 24, 1973.

Probing the Issues

Each of the six points in the Waldheim speech merits discussion by every congregation in America. We select four. How may we as a Christian congregation contribute to the amelioration of the crisis?

Mass poverty. Does our comparative national wealth automatically place us in the realm which James calls *the world?* How can we act instead as heirs of the kingdom vis-à-vis the poor in other nations?

Food. Food is now a scarce commodity, the cost of which increasingly prevents its purchase by the hungry. Should American Christians reduce their own consumption of food? Should they contribute more to agencies such as Church World Service? Should they pressure the Federal Government to set aside a tithe of its exportable food for distribution in famine and flood regions? Should they continue to feed their pets more food than human beings have to eat in India or Pakistan?

Energy. America consumes a vast disproportion of the planet's supply of energy. What can the churches do to conserve supplies and to reduce consumption? What should be their response to future embargoes of oil (or other raw materials) to the American market?

Military expenditure. The Pentagon annually increases its demands until the American budget for arms is the largest in the world. How can the churches justify their tacit consent to this use of funds, personnel, energy, and raw materials?

Members of the United Nations, at the Special Session in 1974, affirmed their determination to work for "the establishment of a new international economic order, based on equity, sovereign equality, interdependence, common interest and cooperation among all States, irrespective of their economic and social systems which shall correct inequalities and redress existing injustices, make it possible to eliminate the widening gap between the developed and the developing countries and ensure steadily accelerating economic and social development in peace and justice for present and future generations." In what ways can American churches, working with sister churches in other countries, contribute to the realization of such an aim? Since the United States is one of the developed countries whose self-interest may prompt it to oppose a "new order" of this kind, what should American churches do when that opposition emerges?

And So, Again to The Letter of James

Today's study illustrates several reasons why many readers conclude that Scripture is no longer applicable to modern problems.

First, James deals with attitudes *within a Christian congregation.* We face difficulties in applying such a text to conditions of wealth and poverty in *secular society as a whole.* Are these difficulties of such a nature that the Scriptural notion of the conflict between the world and the Kingdom of God has become obsolete? Or do the difficulties underscore the relevance of the letter?

Second, James deals with *individual* morality, for example, the attitudes of a poor Christian toward a rich Christian. In the modern period, the struggle between the rich and the poor takes place on a national level, for example, in the shaping of federal legislation controlling industrial competition, minimum wages, and welfare policies. Has the distance between a first-century Christian congregation and the twentieth-century Congress of the United States become too great to be bridged by the teaching of James?

Third, the decisive issues today have to do with the relations of *rich nations* to *poor nations* in such complex matters as the control of raw materials, the pricing of export commodities, the fluctuation of currencies. Do the words of James retain any sense when applied to such problems as those faced by the United Nations? If so, how can the teaching of James be translated into international programs?

More is at stake here than simply holding on to a private moral teaching on the part of James. More was at stake for James than hunger and destitution. What is at stake is God, his Kingdom, Christ as the Lord of glory, and the validity of his royal law. If we declare James irrelevant, can we salvage anything at all from "the faith of our Lord Jesus Christ" that is applicable to the wealth and poverty of nations?

Supplementary Reading

On the Scripture

Blackman, Edwin Cyril, *The Epistle of James* (Torch Bible Commentaries) (Alec R. Allenson, Inc., 1957), pp. 75–89.

Minear, Paul S., *Commands of Christ* (Abingdon Press, 1972), Chs. 4–6.

Mitton, Charles Leslie, *The Epistle of James* (London: Marshall, Morgan & Scott, Ltd., 1966), pp. 80–98.

On the Issue

Limits to Growth: Report of the Club of Rome (Universe Books, 1972).

From National Council of Churches, Church World Service, Room 678, 475 Riverside Drive, New York, N.Y. 10027, publications on world hunger.

Simon, Paul and Arthur, *The Politics of World Hunger* (Harper & Row Publishers, Inc., 1973).

From the United Nations, *Proceedings of the World*

Food Conference, November 1974, in Rome: United Nations, 1st Avenue at 42d Street, New York, N.Y. 10017.

The U.S. and the Developing World: Agenda for Action 1974 (Praeger Publishers). This annual publication of the Overseas Development Council will probably be available in a later edition.

For up-to-date material on world hunger and on efforts to reduce the ranks of the starving, groups should consult the *Readers' Guide to Periodical Literature.*

On the Security-Obsession

The Scripture: Hebrews 11:24–38; 12:1–3

(Consult the Revised Standard Version or the New American Bible.)

The Discovery: Persecution produces the greatest security

This Christian author had his own obsession. He was obsessed above all with the story of Jesus as "the pioneer and perfecter of our faith," and obsessed by the discovery that the pain and shame of the cross was the mysterious clue to the glory and joy of Jesus. Pondering the story of Jesus as disclosing a pattern of behavior, this author discovered many earlier illustrations of the pattern in the long line of pilgrims who had received security by way of persecution, a line beginning as early as Abel (11:4). Moses was another pioneer whose faith had enabled him to "conquer kingdoms" by suffering ill-treatment. Hebrews presents Jesus as the pattern of all pioneering as well as the Perfecter of all pioneers, since they had all pointed directly toward him. Because he is the pattern, true faith can be found only where a pilgrim relies on the Jesus-kind of security by "wandering over deserts and mountains, and in dens and caves of the earth." Faith changes to sin whenever the pilgrim gets weary or fainthearted (12:3), whenever he seeks the world's kind of security. So this faith is to be detected not in words but in people, in their courage under fire, their patience under duress. God there gives them one kind of security; the world tempts them with another.

What a remarkable gallery of portraits in Heb., ch. 11! The saga covers many generations; pilgrims are photographed in many postures: Moses' parents hiding him in the reeds of the swamp; Moses himself leaving the secure haven of the Pharaoh's palace; refugees venturing into the waters of the Red Sea; crazy trumpeters marching around thick Jericho walls; imprisoned prophets sealing the mouths of hungry lions; women mourning the deaths of their children. The author glimpses analogies in every conceivable type of person: young and old, male and female, famous and anonymous. He shows how every situation posed the same basic temptation (the world's promise of lower risk) and the same basic opportunity (God's promise of something better though at higher risk). He warned every Christian that he was being watched, not by the FBI or CIA, but by this whole gallery of pilgrims (12:1). The substance of faith is to become worthy of them; the world's promise of security applies only to those who cop out of this procession.

The saga permits us various glimpses of the world's kind of security: to live as Pharaoh's grandson; to gain the treasures of Egypt; to have the favor of the king; to be guarded by the armies of the empire; to be safe within the walls of Jericho; to share the strength of lions and the protection of "maximum-security prisons." Should we add the wealth of millionaires, listings in *Who's Who,* awards of Oscars and Nobel prizes? As this author weighed the alternatives, to seek rewards of this sort made people worthy of the world; to spurn them made them pilgrims "of whom the world was not worthy." The world is obsessed with one sort of security; the pilgrim with another.

Even Christians who are hardened to Scripture may be shocked when they confront the harsh choice between these two obsessions. They eagerly look for some softening of the options. This may induce them to discount this author's "martyr complex" as a pathological product of ancient persecution, which fortunately is no longer current. Yet Jesus himself barred this escape, for he declared equally rugged choices. The Gospels are just as ruthless in requiring every disciple to sacrifice "house or brothers or sisters or mother or father or children or lands" (Mark 10:29). He must accept separation from family (Luke 12:52–53), must sell his possessions (Luke 12:33), must reject "treasures on earth" (Matt. 6:19), must accept persecution (Matt. 5:10–11), and in fact take up his cross and lose his life (Mark 8:34–35). Indeed, every major writer in the New Testament accepts the sufferings of Christ as providing the pattern and the power for the disciples to suffer. Baptism and Eucharist comprise their pledge to participate in his dying. No, more than this—they celebrate that very participation, their dying with him. Their vocation is to carry "in the body the death of Jesus, so that the life of Jesus may also be manifested in our bodies" (II Cor. 4:10).

The New Testament speaks with one voice on this matter: idolatry is simply the desire for another kind of security, the kind that the world makes so alluring. The worship of false gods is masked by this desire. Today the world is itself obsessed with the need for security. It seeks the security of wealth, and banks provide the cathedrals for this worship. Since financial security is dependent on national and international trade and currencies, each individual bank is a tiny part of the interlocking structures of international conglomerates. The world desires security for the family, and what a universe takes shape around the care and nurture of that desire! A fantastically complex realm of insurances—health, medical, automobile, homeowners', life, and annuity—are only as good as the investment and exchange systems, with daily fluctuations in the value of such "securities."

The world desires the security of the nation, and what a labyrinth of activities that desire has spawned! Military forces, nuclear stockpiles, international trade in armaments; economies pegged to the prospering of war industries; excitements and impasses in diplomatic negotiations; coups and civil wars; wars of independence and wars of suppression; the formation of larger and larger international blocs, with the purchased support of puppet regimes; the proliferation of national security councils and agencies, the CIA, FBI, and spying from satellites. Never in human history has the desire for national security been so dominant as today. No wonder that this single obsession seems to provide the clearest, sharpest, most extreme antithesis in America to the security-obsession of the author of Hebrews. No wonder that many American church members, should they be forced to choose between national security and allegiance to Christ, would unhesitatingly choose the first. Because of this, they use every avail-

able precaution to avoid situations in which they might
be forced to make that choice. In that precaution the
author of Hebrews would recognize already a copping
out from the procession of pilgrims.

Voices of Alarm

Ever since World War II we have had in the U.S.A.,
not crazy men calling "Fire!" in crowded theaters, but
politicians crying "National Security" in a crowded international world. Actually this obsession with the
security of the nation is a quite recent phenomenon.
When and why have we become so apprehensive about
the future? The growth of these paranoiac fears has
accompanied the growth of American imperial power,
step by step. The more extensive our empire, the more
massive our atomic stockpiles, the more complex the
Pentagon bureaucracy, the longer the chain of military
installations around the world—the more nervous we
become. And rightly so, since the more we rely upon
such methods of defense, the more vulnerable and frag-
ile the entire system.

National security serves as the justification for all
sorts of un-American corruptions: for destruction of
natural resources, both here and abroad; for deceiving
not only the public but nonmilitary echelons of government; for unlimited surveillance of citizens; for foment-
ing revolutions and buying governments abroad; for
imprisoning or exiling thousands of dissidents; for building and staffing military installations rather than famine
relief; for continual modernization of methods for de-
stroying the planet. America has become its own worst
enemy, bound to perish by its own sword; or, to use

more apt idioms, to breathe its own nerve gasses and to watch its cities shrivel in atomic holocaust.

1974. EGIL KROGH, JR.

I have throughout this most difficult period been free, first because I had not yet been indicted and later because I had been released on my own recognizance. And I perceive this freedom as the very essence of our society and our system.

This freedom for me is not a privilege but a right protected by our Constitution. It is one of a host of rights that I as an American citizen am fortunate to share with Dr. Ellsberg and Dr. Fielding. These rights of the individual cannot be sacrificed to the mere assertion of national security.

National security is obviously a fundamental goal and a proper concern of any country. It is also a concept that is subject to a wide range of definitions. . . .

But however national security is defined, I now see that none of the potential uses of the sought information could justify the invasion of the rights of the individuals that the break-in necessitated. . . . These rights are the definition of our nation. To invade them unlawfully in the name of national security is to work a destructive force upon the nation, not to take a protective measure. . . .

The sincerity of my motivation was not a justification but indeed a contributing cause of the incident. I hope that the young men and women who are fortunate enough to have an opportunity to serve in government can benefit from this experi-

ence and learn that sincerity can often be as blind-
ing as it is worthy. I hope they will recognize that
the banner of national security can turn perceived
patriotism into actual disservice. When contem-
plating a course of action, I hope they will never
fail to ask, "Is this right?"

Egil Krogh, Jr., after U.S. District Court
sentence, in *The New York Times*,
January 24, 1974.

1961. THE THIRD ASSEMBLY, WORLD COUNCIL OF CHURCHES

War is contrary to the will of God. War in its
newer forms is understood not only by Christians but by the general conscience of the nations as an offence against both the world of nature and the race of man, threatening
annihilation and laying on mankind an unbeara-
ble burden of cost and terror. The use of indis-
criminate weapons must now be condemned by
the churches as an affront to the Creator and a
denial of the very purposes of the Creation.
Christians must refuse to place their ultimate
trust in war and nuclear weapons. . . . The use
of nuclear weapons, or other forms of major vio-
lence, against centres of population is in no circumstances reconcilable with the demands of
the Christian Gospel.

World Council of Churches, *New Delhi Speaks*
(London: SCM Press, Ltd., 1962), p. 46.

1965. VATICAN COUNCIL II

The arms race in which so many countries are engaged is not a safe way to preserve a steady peace. Nor is the so-called balance resulting from this race a sure and authentic peace. Rather than being eliminated, thereby, the causes of war threaten to grow gradually stronger. While extravagant sums are being spent for the furnishing of ever new weapons, an adequate remedy cannot be provided for the multiple miseries afflicting the whole modern world. Disagreements between nations are not really and radically healed. On the contrary, other parts of the world are infected with them. . . . The arms race is an utterly treacherous trap for humanity, and one which injures the poor to an intolerable degree. It is much to be feared that if this race persists, it will eventually spawn all the lethal ruin whose path it is now making ready.

Walter M. Abbott and Joseph Gallagher (eds.), *The Documents of Vatican II* (Association Press, 1966), p. 295.

1972. LEONARD BERNSTEIN

O you people of power,
O you people of power, your hour is now.
You may plan to rule forever, but you never do somehow.

So we wait in silent treason until reason is restored
And we wait for the season of the Word of the Lord.
We await the season of the Word of the Lord . . .

From Leonard Bernstein's *Mass.* Copyright 1971 by Leonard Bernstein and Stephen Schwartz. Used by permission of G. Schirmer, Inc.

1974. A NEWSPAPER RELEASE

The request for military spending in the U.S. budget for Fiscal Year 1975 has been set at almost 90 billion dollars.

1900. JOSIAH STRONG

But as the world is gradually being civilized and civilization is gradually being Christianized, armies are finding new occupations. As *The Outlook* says: "The army among Anglo-Saxon peoples is no longer a mere instrument of destruction. It is a great reconstructive organization. It is promoting law, order, civilization, and is fighting famine and pestilence in India. It is lightening taxes, building railroads, laying the foundations of justice and liberty, in Egypt."

Josiah Strong, quoted in Robert T. Handy, *A Christian America* (Oxford University Press, 1971), p. 126.

1962. MELVIN LAIRD

Time, to the extent that we do not use it in furthering our own cause and perfecting our own strengths, buys for the enemy the needed days, months, and years in which to catch up and eventually, if unimpeded, surpass us. . . . In the next few years, conceivably, we could move into the perilous phase of nuclear parity. . . . We must serve credible notice "that we reserve to ourselves the initiative to strike first when the Soviet peril point rises beyond its tolerable limit." Nor can the technological superiority that we now possess give us much comfort. In the name of all that is holy, we must continue to move ahead ceaselessly: our margin *"cannot protect us from technological breakthroughs!"* (Laird's italics) . . . To support this national purpose, a strong domestic economy, a strong standing military force, and advances in weapons systems are required. Civilization and the urban ethos, indeed, God's will, demand them.

Melvin Laird, quoted in Max Stackhouse, *The Ethics of Necropolis* (Beacon Press, Inc., 1971), pp. 85–86.

Probing the Issues

—Before entering into a discussion, each member of the group may be asked to add his voice to those which have been quoted above by completing the following two sentences:

1. As a Christian, I believe that the security of America consists primarily of . . .

2. This congregation can contribute to national security primarily by the following actions: . . .

The discussion may then proceed by an attempt to pool the various sentences into one statement.

—Today, in the discussion of the forces that constitute the greatest threat to the survival of mankind, there are many who label as Threat No. 1 the unchallenged power of the military-industrial complex in the U.S.A. Simultaneously, in current discussion of threats to national security, there are many who label as Threat No. 1 the growing reliance upon such international agencies as the

United Nations. Which of these threats should
American churches take more seriously? Why?

—In the response to the Confession of 1967 of the
United Presbyterian Church, the following sentence has been hotly debated. How would your
congregation line up in this debate?

> The search for cooperation and peace . . . re-
> quires that the nations pursue fresh and responsi-
> ble relations across every line of conflict, *even at
> risk to national security,* to reduce areas of strife
> and to broaden international understanding.
>
> Confession of 1967, Part II, Sec. A, 4b
> (italics added).

—In the Pentagon Papers case, the need for national
security was cited to justify widespread spying on
civilians, including the invasion of the office of Ellsberg's psychiatrist. A key person in that invasion
was Egil Krogh, Jr., whose statement is cited above.
Evaluate the changes in his conception of patriotism before and after his trial.

Visiting Again the Hebrews Gallery of Pilgrim Portraits

After writing the above sections, I have gone back to
Heb., ch. 11, and have read it again. Then I have asked
myself this question: During the past few years, which
Americans have the best credentials for being included
in that list of pilgrims, credentials that indicate the kind
of security and freedom which those pilgrims dis-
played? The first three names that popped into my
mind were these: Martin Luther King, Jr., Daniel Berri-

gan, S.J., William Stringfellow. I need not here mount
a defense for those names, but I suggest that each
reader of Heb., ch. 11, should complete the list of pilgrims by including his own nominees. Let the discussion group attempt this. This will force a review of
Heb., ch. 11, to locate the criteria for including heroes.
Also relevant is our study of Matt., ch. 23, in Study 2.
(Note that the nearer the author of Hebrews came to
his own epoch, the more general his description and
the more anonymous the list.)

At every celebration of the Eucharist, the original
meaning of Jesus' sacrifice might be recovered by reading this section of Hebrews, with its climactic vision of
Jesus in 12:1–2 and its appeal to courage on the part of
his followers in 12:3. So this Scripture might well be
"The Word of the Lord" read at the next Eucharist in
your church. With this in mind, let the group listen to
the music of Bernstein's *Mass* (Side 2, Section VIII,
"The Word of the Lord"), and then discuss whether the
composer has succeeded in expressing an authentic up-
dating of Scripture.

In America the church has not been subject to wide-
scale persecution; this fact may disqualify us from understanding Hebrews. We need the testimony of Christians from other countries who "escaped the edge of
the sword, won strength out of weakness," Christians
from Nazi Germany, Communist Czechoslovakia,
apartheid South Africa; from countries under military
juntas, such as Brazil and Chile. This testimony comes
to us in part through the ecumenical agencies, for only
Christians from other nations can disclose our own
idolatrous nationalisms. That is why the declarations of
such agencies as the World Council of Churches should
be taken as serious efforts to translate the implications

of letters such as Hebrews into conciliar letters for
U.S.A. churches.

Hebrews depicts a most strenuous kind of life as normal for Christians. Why, considering the character of
salvation, should this be so? Is the lowering of the cost
of discipleship perhaps our greatest treason?

Supplementary Reading

On the Scripture

Calvin, John, *Commentaries on the Epistle of Paul the
Apostle to the Hebrews,* tr. and ed. by John Owen
(Wm. B. Eerdmans Publishing Company, 1948), pp.
292–313.

Montefiore, Hugh W., *The Epistle to the Hebrews* (London: Adam & Charles Black, Ltd., 1964), pp. 201–
217.

Neil, William, *The Epistle to the Hebrews* (London:
SCM Press, Ltd., 1955), pp. 116–128.

On the Issues

Abbott, Walter M., and Gallagher, Joseph (eds.), "Constitution on the Church in the Modern World," in *The
Documents of Vatican II* (Association Press, 1966).

Kierkegaard, Søren, *Gospel of Suffering* (Augsburg
Publishing House, 1948).

World Council of Churches, *New Delhi Speaks* (London: SCM Press, Ltd., 1962), section on Service.

STUDY 9

The Struggle Against Invisible Forces

The Scripture: I Corinthians 2:6–8; 15:20–26

(Consult the Revised Standard Version.)

The Discovery: Good Friday is the symbol of God's war; Easter is the symbol of his peace

God has declared war and has sent his Son with a sword. Therefore it becomes absolutely essential to recognize who his enemies are. Against whom does Christ fight in the name of God? One answer is given in story form, a story that is etched on the brain of every Christian, the story of Jesus' death. This is the Good Friday declaration of war (Matt., chs. 26 and 27; Mark, chs. 14 and 15; Luke, chs. 22 and 23; John, chs. 18 and 19). Who killed this man? When Paul attempts to answer that question, he says, "The rulers of this age." (I Cor. 2:8.) Who, then, are these rulers who are "doomed to pass away"? As the adversaries of Christ, they presumably remain the adversaries of his followers. Who are they?

Paul gives certain clues. They are rulers of *this age.* To locate the boundaries of the age is to locate its rulers.

This age is coextensive with a kind of wisdom, the wisdom of men, which cannot comprehend the secret hidden wisdom of God. It was this kind of wisdom which led men to crucify Jesus, wisdom which saw in the cross nothing but foolishness and weakness. The two ages are separated by two competing kinds of power and wisdom. This clue leads us to suspect that the enemies of God were not individual persons as much as this power, this wisdom, which had established control over minds and hearts. The Passion Story as told in all four Gospels supports this understanding of these enemies.

In Luke, Jesus tells his captors, "This is your hour, and the *power of darkness.*" (Luke 22:53, italics added.) According to all four Gospels, Jesus is crucified as a king by men who protest their innocence. As a king he is seen as a threat to every other form of government, whether political or religious. Barabbas, a revolutionary leader, is considered less dangerous than this other criminal. All actors in the story share some degree of responsibility and guilt: the Romans, the priests and elders, the bystanders, but especially the disciples themselves. The Gospel of John makes it clear that Pilate operates under a higher authority, and that the issue is between a kingship "of this world" and a kingship "not of this world" (John 18:36). If the men of power in this world had known the true power of this condemned man, they would not have crucified him. So says Paul, and John makes Pilate's ignorance of that power entirely clear. The true rulers of this age are invisible forces embodied in notions of wisdom and power. Not Pilate and Rome, but Roman national*ism*, and imperial*ism;* not Sadducees and Pharisees, but religious institutional*ism* and professional*ism;* not the disciples, but their belief that Jesus' enemies were stronger and wiser than he, and the actions of betrayal, denial, and flight which expressed those beliefs. The mark of all these enmities—death. . . . The measure of their sin was his death.

In I Cor. 15:26 Paul recognizes in death "the last enemy"; but he also identifies the other enemies—"every rule and every authority and power," which had used his death to protect their jurisdiction (v. 24). Easter declares that God has put all these enemies under Jesus' feet. Note that Paul does not here mention as enemies Pilate, the Romans, the religious authorities, or even Paul's own violent opposition (v. 9). He was not a person to minimize the guilt of any of these men; but he knew that only if Christ had won a victory over the wise and powerful "rulers of this age," and only if he had overcome the death which they could inflict, only so could the resurrection of Christ bring salvation to all humanity. Only when every such ruler is overcome can God become "everything to every one" (v. 28). Until that time any reliance by any Christian on the wisdom of this age simply empties Christ's cross of its power (1:17). We can summarize the Bible study as follows:

1. Not the nation, but nationalism is the enemy of God; to exalt or to fear the power and wisdom of the nation is to crucify Christ afresh.

2. Not the nation, but nationalism is defeated by the resurrection of Christ; faith in the risen Lord frees people from the wisdom and power of the rulers of this age.

The Voices Behind the Voices

Who are these rulers? Various scholars point to an answer.

1972. JOHN H. YODER

. . . We might say that we have here an inclusive vision of religious structures (especially the religious undergirdings of stable ancient and primitive societies), intellectual structures (ologies and isms), moral structures (codes and customs), political structures (the tyrant, the market, the school, the courts, race and nation). . . .

All these structures can be conceived of in their general essence as parts of a good creation. There could not be society or history, there could not be Man without the existence above him of religious, intellectual, moral and social structures. *We cannot live without them. . . .*

But these structures fail to serve man as they should. They do not enable him to live a genuinely free, human, loving life. They have absolutized themselves and they demand from the individual and society an unconditional loyalty. They harm and enslave man. *We cannot live with them. . . .*

If, then, God is going to save man *in his humanity*, the Powers cannot simply be destroyed or set aside or ignored. Their sovereignty must be broken. This is what Jesus did, concretely and historically, by living among men a genuinely free and human existence. This life brought him, as any genuinely human existence will bring any man, to the cross. In his death the Powers—in this case the most worthy, weighty representatives of Jewish religion and Roman politics—acted in collusion. Like all men, he too was subject (but in his case quite willingly) to these powers. He accepted his own status of submission. But morally he broke their rules by refusing to support them in their self-glorification, and that is why they killed him. . . .

This they did in order to avoid the threat to their dominion represented by the very fact that he existed in their midst so morally independent of their pretensions. He did not fear even death. Therefore his cross is a victory.

John H. Yoder, *The Politics of Jesus* (Wm. B. Eerdmans Publishing Company, 1972), pp. 145–148.

1962. HENDRIK BERKHOF

If this victory over the powers constitutes the work of Christ, then it must be also a message for the church to proclaim. "To me, less than the least of all the saints," says Paul, "was given the grace to proclaim among the Gentiles the gospel of the inscrutable riches of Christ . . . so that the manifold wisdom of God should henceforth be made known by means of the church to the principalities and powers in heavenly places." (Eph. 3:8–10)

Paul's statement is made in connection with the truth that since Christ a new force has made its entry on the stage of salvation history: the church. . . . She is an undreamed synthesis of the two sorts of men who people the world, Jews and Gentiles. That Christ has brought together both into one body is the mystery, which for ages had remained hidden (v. 9) but has come to light, thanks to Paul's ministry. . . .

This is what the church announces to the Powers. The very existence of the church, in which

Gentiles and Jews . . . live together in Christ's fellowship, is itself a proclamation . . . to the Powers that their unbroken dominion has come to an end.

This same fact is also freighted with meaning for the Christians. All resistance and every attack against the gods of this age will be unfruitful, unless the church herself is resistance and attack, unless she demonstrates in her life and fellowship how men can live freed from the Powers. We can only preach the manifold wisdom of God to Mammon if our life displays that we are joyfully freed from his clutches. To reject nationalism we must begin by no longer recognizing in our own bosoms any difference between peoples.

> Hendrik Berkhof, *Christ and the Powers*
> (Herald Press, 1962), pp. 41 f.

1973. WILLIAM STRINGFELLOW

A biblical person is always wary of claims which the State makes for allegiance, obedience and service under the rubric called patriotism. Such demands are often put in noble or benign or innocuous terms. But in any country the rhetoric and rituals of conformity and obedience to a regime or ruler latently concern idolatry of the Antichrist, even though that name is not generally invoked except where the explicit and blatant deification of the State occurs.

Where that happens, the magnitude of the malevolence of the Antichrist for both God and human beings, specifically those who refuse to renounce their humanity and become idolators of

death, is exposed. Where that takes place, the State
or principality as Antichrist is also revealed as a
grotesque parody of Jesus Christ and of his Church
in the vocation of the holy nation. Where that
comes to pass, the State as Antichrist persecutes or
subverts, supersedes and seeks to displace the
Church of Christ, even as the Antichrist tries to
tempt Christ or entrap Christ, or condemn Christ
or mock Christ or crucify Christ or overthrow the
Lordship of Christ or insinuate that the Antichrist
is Christ. In such days, which in some sense are
always these days, the churchly institutions are
banished or destroyed or converted into function-
aries of the State. Those human beings and communities of humans who persevere in fidelity to
God and to the gift of their humanity, those who
resist death and thus live in Jesus Christ—whether
that be a public formality or not—do so under the
condemnation of the State in one way or another,
be it ridicule and ostracism, in poverty or imprisonment, as sojourners or fugitives, in clandestine existence, as a confessing movement, or, otherwise, in
resistance. . . .

The American vanity as a nation has, since the
origins of America, been Babylonian—boasting,
through Presidents, often through pharisees within
the churches, through folk religion, and in other
ways, that America is Jerusalem. This is neither an
innocuous nor benign claim; it is the essence of the
doctrine of the Antichrist.

William Stringfellow, *An Ethic for Christians
and Other Aliens in a Strange Land* (Word,
Inc., 1973), pp. 113–114.

1974. FREDERICK HERZOG

Invisible forces should not be identified solely with nationalism. I'd like to see more of the "web" of forces exposed: nationalism ties in with capitalism, also with individualism . . . (with) all dimensions of a misconceived way of life. . . . What seems to be required today is a changing of the American's inner eyes. . . . We rearrange the mental furniture, reshuffle our concepts, but don't get inner eyes, those eyes with which we look through our physical eyes upon reality.

> Frederick Herzog, Letter to Paul S. Minear,
> June 2, 1974.

1974. AL CARMINES

Only a few months ago "Honor America" Days and "Support Our President" Rallies proliferated, manned by boozed-out entertainers, their cynical smiles painted on their public relations faces, their hands arched in a perpetual salute to an America that would have made Thomas Jefferson retch and Abraham Lincoln weep. Nor has the left presented a more edifying spectacle. Our shining heroes of the anti-war movement and the new revolution now daze their minds with drugs and religion in a grotesque caricature of the very forces in America they once despised. . . . And the great moderate, liberal mass of concerned Americans flock to the issues of environmental control and consumer protection as if those issues are . . . neutral enough to spare us the cynicism and disillusionment which every other political and social crusade has finally engendered. . . .

The goal of the Gospel is finally not to make us feel good in the way we feel good in the womb—no problems, curled up in a state of bliss; the goal of the Gospel is the experience not of avoiding our anxiety but grasping it, seeing through it the heart of a God who asks us to be grownups, not children; to strive for real goals, not imaginary chimeras; to love real people, not fantasies of them. . . .

That Gospel disturbs our pride and brings us up short, but it finally gives us the most solid and real comfort available in this world. It truly comforts us because it takes all of us—our weakness and strength—into its accounting. For a radical human condition it proposes a radical remedy—the cross. And for a radical inertia, it proposes a radical change of direction-conversion. And the cross and conversion mean a stepping into reality—faith in God rather than some para-religion called "faith in faith."

Al Carmines, pastor, Judson Memorial Church,
New York City, Sermon preached
on January 20, 1974.

1967. THE UNITED PRESBYTERIAN CHURCH U.S.A.

God's reconciliation in Jesus Christ is the ground of the peace, justice, and freedom among nations which all powers of government are called to serve and defend. The church, in its own life, is called to practice the forgiveness of enemies and to commend to the nations as practical politics the search for cooperation and peace. This search requires that the nations pursue fresh and responsible relations across every line of conflict, even at risk to national security, to reduce areas of strife and to broaden international understanding. Reconciliation among nations becomes peculiarly urgent as countries develop nuclear, chemical, and biological weapons, diverting their manpower and resources from constructive uses and risking the annihilation of mankind. Although nations may serve God's purposes in history, the church which identifies the sovereignty of any one nation or any one way of life with the cause of God denies the Lordship of Christ and betrays its calling.

Confession of 1967, Part II, Section A, 4b.

1974. JÜRGEN MOLTMANN

Without a revolution in the concept of God, there will be no revolutionary faith. Without God's liberation from idolatrous images . . . there will be no liberating theology. . . . As M. Luther said, "Where you put the trust of your heart, that in fact is your God." . . . Which God governs Christian existence—the one who was crucified or the idols of religion, class, race, and society? Without a new clarity in Christian faith itself, there will be no credibility in Christian life.

Jürgen Moltmann, in *Theology Today*, Vol. 31 (1974), pp. 6–7.

Probing the Issues

—In what ways do the stories of Jesus' death help us to detect the enemies of God, and so to arm ourselves against the same enemies?

—How do the voices of contemporary scholars help us to detect the point where loyalty to nation becomes idolatrous nationalism? Where do you locate this point?

—Have these discussions made you *more* or *less* aware of the accuracy of Stringfellow's warning?

—We have heard a great deal about the dangers of the church entering politics. Have we been so alert to the dangers of politics in the church? How does the Pauline analysis of wisdom and power in I Cor., ch. 2, help us to locate the invasion of political ideologies into our Christian thinking?

—Members of the discussion group should be invited to describe situations during the past decade in which Christians have most openly challenged "the rulers of this age." What has been the impact on the churches of each of these challenges? on the nation?

—As the group recalls its various discussions and reflects upon the statement of Professor Moltmann, it may well ask itself how, specifically, it might now free its faith in God from idolatry and thereby enhance the credibility of its Christian life.

—The group should examine the hymnbook to locate the hymns that best express the struggle between Jesus and the powers in his death and the victory over the powers in his resurrection. In what ways are these hymns relevant?

—Analyze two versions of Martin Luther's "A Mighty Fortress Is Our God" to see which is more faithful to the New Testament and which is more applicable to our own churches in America. One version is in the hymnal; a more recent adaptation is found in the Peoples Mass Book:

A mighty fortress is our God, a bulwark never failing,
Protecting us with staff and rod, His power all prevailing.
What if the nations rage and surging seas rampage;
What though the mountains fall, the Lord is God of all
    On earth is not his equal.

The waters of his goodness flow through his holy city,
And gladden hearts of those who know His tenderness
    and pity.
Though nations stand unsure, God's kingdom shall endure;
His power shall remain, His peace shall ever reign,
    Our God, the God of Jacob.

Behold his wondrous deeds of peace, the God of our
    salvation;
He knows our wars and makes them cease in every land
    and nation.
The warrior's spear and lance are splintered by his glance;
The guns and nuclear might stand withered in his sight;
    The Lord of hosts is with us.

Omer Westendorf, based on Martin Luther.
from *Peoples Mass Book* (Cincinnati: World Library
of Sacred Music, Inc. 1964). Copyright, 1964,
World Library Publications, Inc.
Used by permission.

A Return to Dialogue with Paul

In I Cor. 15:25–27 the apostle says *both* that these invisible authorities have already been put under subjection to Christ *and* that during his rule he continues to win victories over them. How does the struggle between the church and nationalist idolatries help us to understand that apparent contradiction?

When we understand death (15:21) as a sign of man's captivity to nationalistic ideologies, what new significance does this give to the Christian celebration every Sunday of Jesus' triumph over death? How does this give the message and the life of the church a relevance to political, economic, and racial conflicts? Paul seems to say that apart from such relevance his faith would be futile (v. 17). Is that true of your faith?

A central theme in Paul's message is the folly and weakness of the cross (1:18–25) and the folly and weakness of those who preach it (2:1–5). Our consideration of the relative power and wisdom of nationalism in the modern world should underscore this theme. Do you think that the evidence of two thousand years of history concerning the strength of nations and the weakness of the churches would lead Paul to change his position in I Corinthians? (The reasons for your answer may be more important than your answer.)

I Cor. 15:58 represents the true conclusion of Paul's treatment of the resurrection, a conclusion that is often neglected. When we understand the resurrection as Christ's victory over such "rulers of this age" as nationalism and popular ideologies, how does this verse become applicable to the work of individual Christians in political and social affairs?

To what extent are members of your church aware that at Easter we celebrate the triumph of God over all such sources of corruption, with death expressing the apparent vulnerability of humanity to corporate vanities and coalitions of powers, such as those which seemed to triumph on Good Friday?

Supplementary Reading

On the Scripture

Barrett, C. K., *The First Epistle to the Corinthians* (Harper's New Testament Commentaries) (Harper & Row, Publishers, Inc., 1968), pp. 66–75, 353–361.

Barth, Karl, *The Resurrection of the Dead* (Fleming H. Revell Company, 1933).

Caird, George B., *Principalities and Powers* (Oxford: Clarendon Press, 1956).

Craig, Clarence Tucker, and Short, John, "The First Epistle to the Corinthians," *The Interpreter's Bible* (Abingdon Press, 1953), Vol. X, pp. 35–42, 222–240.

On the Invisible Powers

Hamilton, Kenneth, *To Turn from Idols* (Wm. B. Eerdmans Publishing Company, 1973).

Minear, Paul S., *I Saw a New Earth* (Corpus Instrumentorum, Inc., 1968).

Stringfellow, William, *An Ethic for Christians and Other Aliens in a Strange Land* (Word, Inc., 1973).

Swomley, John M., Jr., *Liberation Ethics* (The Macmillan Company, 1972), Ch. 3.

Yoder, John H., *The Politics of Jesus* (Wm. B. Eerdmans Publishing Company, 1972).

A CLOSING HYMN

Christian, dost thou see them
  On the holy ground,
How the powers of darkness
  Compass thee around?

Christian, up and smite them,
  Counting gain but loss,
In the strength that cometh
  By the holy cross.

. . . .

Christian, dost thou hear them,
  How they speak thee fair,
"Always fast and vigil,
  Always watch and prayer?"

Christian, answer boldly,
  "While I breathe, I pray!"
Peace shall follow battle;
  Night shall end in day.

St. Andrew of Crete (ca. 660– ca. 732), *Pilgrim Hymnal* (The Pilgrim Press, 1958), No. 364.